Asset Title & Liens for Investors

Trust + Equity Secrets

JAMES BILLINGS

Asset Title & Liens for Investors – Trust + Equity Secrets

Author: James Billings
Book design: Victor Hernandez

First Edition. 2024. San Diego, California USA

Published by TA Media Trust

Cover Images:
Royal Courts of Justice 2019. By David Castor. Public domain.
Royal Courts of Justice Sign. By The Lud. Public domain.

ISBN:
978-1-7322048-3-6

Contact:
cs@trustarte.com
+1 619 537 8625
trustarte.com
youtube.com/@TrustArte

Also from the Author:

The Uncorporation: Unleashing the Power of the Business Trust for Your Protection and Privacy

CONTENTS

PERSONAL PROPERTY

DEDICATIONS

This book is dedicated to Richard who taught me to 'look for what's missing', and to Jack who taught me to 'out-think the other guy.'

INTRODUCTION

This is a book about asset title and liens for investors.

Generally when most people hear "title" they think about ownership. For example, the owner of real estate, a vehicle or a bank account.

But title is far more expansive because there are two distinct components. One is 'legal' and the other is 'equitable.' Legal is the name on a deed or any type of ownership document. Equitable is the right to enjoy or secure various benefits.

A "lien" is a claim against one or more assets of a property owner. This lien can attach to the real property (real estate) or personal property (bank account, vehicle, equipment).

Specific liens are voluntary such as a home loan. General liens are involuntary such as the case of tax obligations or a civil judgment.

And then we have vesting. What's that? It's how you (the owner) hold legal title. For example, an unmarried man, a married couple, a business organization, a trust, etc.

The history of title, liens and vesting is a fascinating read. Each one can impact your business, personal investments, or estate planning.

As a securities professional in my early career and later a real estate broker mid-career I observed that many clients are rarely informed about how they hold title. If you ask the brokerage account representative or escrow officer about title vesting they automatically refer you to a booklet or a lawyer.

I've always wanted to write this book because title is often a shallow and quick decision for many people. "How does everybody else do it?" People know it's important but often miss the long-term impacts at their peril.

Stop for a moment and consider the enormous impact title can have on your assets. It can affect your spouse, family, business partners, etc. Not only today but in the event of financial distress, divorce, after death, etc.

This book is designed to help you understand the implications of title. In addition, I'll share with you the hidden effect and strategies of equitable liens.

Let's start with an overview of title history. Since land came long before vehicles, banking and technology, we'll begin with real estate. For over two millennia land was always the most important asset anyone could own. We'll explore the origins and evolution of estates, laws, and title.

Aside from ownership itself, ask yourself how could title impact your goals. What alternative vesting might be safer or offer you an advantage?

Examples: For estate planning you might use a living trust for your personal residence or bank accounts. For privacy you might use a land trust for real estate. For limited liability you might use an LLC. For asset protection or anonymity you might use a Business Trust for operations.

You will see how to leverage equitable title to avoid the consequences of legal title transfers. Trusts offer unique stealthy solutions to avoid transfer taxes such as LA's measure ULA aka "Mansion Tax," or stamp duty in the UK and Singapore. These are secrets few know how to execute.

Every time you buy or sell something there is always legal title transfer. When it's a café your evidence is a receipt. When it's a vehicle your evidence is the bill of sale. When it's real estate your evidence is a deed. These all confirm a transfer record.

We begin this book with history then move onto deeper and more descriptive aspects of title elements.

Use this book as a reference guide. It will come in handy as you buy and sell assets over your lifetime. Reach out to us for any questions.

1
TITLE HISTORY IN NORTH AMERICA

The origin of "title" in the context of land ownership has deep historical roots. Initially, in North America, lands were inhabited by Native American tribes who did not practice land ownership as it is understood today. They acknowledged specific rights for fishing and hunting within their tribal territories, but the idea of owning land was foreign to them. This way of life was not exclusive to Native Americans; it mirrored the existence of early hunter-gatherers globally, who depended on the natural world for sustenance and shelter, moving across territories in search of food. In some years, they reaped the benefits of abundant resources, while in others, they faced scarcity.

The transformation began with the advent of agriculture, as ancient peoples learned to dam streams for irrigation, cultivating crops that attracted the wildlife they once hunted. This advancement led to the domestication of animals, securing a stable food supply not subject to the uncertainties of hunting or seasonal changes.

However, this agricultural revolution brought new challenges. The concentration of a consistent food supply in one place necessitated the defense of these valuable lands, giving rise to the concept of land ownership. The idea emerged that those who did not cultivate their own lands might threaten the livelihood of those who did. Communities realized the necessity of having both cultivators to manage the food supply and warriors to protect it, in exchange for a share of the produce.

As societies evolved, agricultural practices improved, leading to surplus production. This surplus was stored, initially in caves and later in more structured warehouses, teaching early societies the importance of saving for future scarcity—a concept echoed in the biblical story of Joseph.

Settlements gradually transitioned from temporary camps to permanent villages, with the construction of durable housing around these storage sites. The need to protect stored supplies and residences led to the establishment of defenders, supported by contributions from the community, laying the groundwork for property rights and taxation. The concept of 'rights in property' came into being along with taxation.

This level of cooperation necessitated a structured social organization to acknowledge and reward the roles of those tending to property and those defending the society. The establishment of recognized rights, along with a system of penalties and rewards, marked the beginnings of governance and political structures.

Over time, societies that mastered the art of cooperation and surplus production engaged in trade, expanding their territories and wealth. This led to larger farms, increased land ownership, and a concentration of economic and military power among the most prosperous tribes, shaping the early dynamics of property ownership and societal organization.

Territorial Conflicts

As humanity evolved from its primal state, tribes formed that often clashed over coveted tracts of land for hunting. The concept of individual land ownership began with an early leader who, wielding authority and a club, claimed the expansive lands from the riverbanks to the distant mountains as his own. This practice of asserting dominion over land through strength became widespread. As societies moved from nomadic ways to settled living across the globe, the powerful seized lands by might, laying the groundwork for the property rights we recognize today. Over time, guided by self-interest, the idea of personal land ownership crystallized into the foundational structure of kingdoms, complete with hierarchical land divisions and feudal systems. This model influenced the development of land ownership in the American colonies, reflecting a long history of land being claimed and governed through power.

2
VALUE ADDED TO LAND CREATES RIGHTS

Transitioning from early land ownership concepts to formalized property rights was a natural progression. Those who actively cultivated the land, whether through farming or ranching, or who constructed durable buildings, were eventually recognized with permanent rights to use, occupy, and possess such lands. This acknowledgment often came in exchange for additional taxes or as a reward for outstanding service in defending these lands or expanding territories, whether through negotiation or conflict. In the United States, this evolution in land ownership and rights was exemplified by landmark legislation such as the Homestead Act, which granted land to settlers willing to cultivate it, and the GI Bill of Rights, providing benefits, including housing assistance, to veterans. These acts underscored the principle that dedication to and investment in the land merited legal and lasting ownership rights.

"...dedication to and investment in the land merited legal and lasting ownership rights."

In the formation of early societies, those who owned property and contributed significantly through taxes, as well as those who played key roles in defending communal lands, often held considerable influence over communal decisions. As these societies evolved, the notion of individual property rights began to overshadow the communal or tribal approach to land ownership. This shift facilitated the accumulation of personal wealth which in turn became a means of exerting power and influence. Wealthy individuals leveraged their resources to gain advantages over those with fewer assets, marking a pivotal transformation in social dynamics and laying the groundwork for more stratified communities.

With the advent of civilization, the complexity of managing and distributing resources like land and water necessitated the development of formal systems to address disputes regarding property rights among community members. This era marked the beginning of recorded ownership, where proof of one's claim to property became essential, not just for transactions such as buying or selling land but also for personal agreements, including marriage dowries and inheritance. Consequently, the institution of legal marriage emerged as a means to clearly define and recognize legal heirs, ensuring that property rights could be accurately passed down through generations. This evolution highlighted the growing need for structured legal frameworks to govern the ownership, inheritance, and exchange of property.

> "...the institution of legal marriage emerged as a means to clearly define and recognize legal heirs, ensuring that property rights could be accurately passed down through generations."

As societies grew more complex, the necessity for concrete and reliable proof of property ownership became paramount. Such documentation needed to possess several key characteristics: it had to be unchallengeable, legally defensible, widely recognized and respected within the community, durable over long periods, easily transferable between parties, and clear to all who read it. This set of requirements led to the innovation and adoption of writing and written records. Initially, inscriptions were made on stone, which, while durable, was not easily transferable. The quest for more practical mediums led to the use of clay tablets, which were followed by papyrus and, eventually, paper. Each advancement in the medium for these records improved upon the last, making the documentation of ownership and other legal matters more accessible and efficient, fundamentally transforming the administration of law, commerce, and society at large.

3
LEGAL RIGHTS REQUIRE A SYSTEM OF ENFORCED LAWS

To ensure the continuity of property rights across generations, societies recognized the need for enduring institutions capable of overseeing and legitimizing these rights beyond the lives of their initial holders. This necessity gave rise to a transformation where the most substantial property owners evolved into influential figures and employers, eventually ascending to the position of King. Over time, these leaders established ruling dynasties and judicial systems tasked with the validation and ongoing confirmation of land ownership rights, all in accordance with societal norms and legal frameworks deemed to be just and equitable.

> "...legal title—a formal recognition and codification of ownership rights to land and property improvements, validated by societal institutions and laws."

This development marked the birth of what is known today as legal title—a formal recognition and codification of ownership rights to land and property improvements, validated by societal institutions and laws. Through this evolution, LEGAL TITLE became a cornerstone of property law, ensuring the stable transfer and recognition of ownership rights through structured legal processes.

The concept of property rights, once consolidated, came to be known as REAL ESTATE or realty, a term originally implying ownership by the monarchy or ruling authority. The validation of land ownership depended on recognition by the sovereign ruler of the territory or nation. Consequently, shifts in rulership or the nation's status often precipitated changes in property ownership and the legal titles associated with real estate.

This arrangement served dual functions:

Firstly, it ensured steadfast allegiance to the monarch and the established government from those whose land ownership was tied to the ruler's favor and tenure. The stability of one's title to land was directly linked to their loyalty and service to the crown.

Secondly, it provided a mechanism for rulers to incentivize and reward military personnel and explorers who played pivotal roles in expanding the realm's territories. Through conquest, treaties, discoveries, or the development of new lands, these individuals could be compensated with a portion of the lands seized, essentially sharing in the "plunder."

This aspect of title law, rewarding expansion and loyalty with land, underpins the historical foundation of legal title to real estate in North America, reflecting a blend of governance, reward, and the strategic expansion of territory.

For nearly three centuries leading up to the Monroe Doctrine of 1823, the imperial powers of Europe—including the Tsars of Russia, and the monarchs of Holland, Spain, Portugal, England, and France—endorsed explorers, ranging from the earliest adventurers to leaders of the American Revolution, to annex lands in America for their respective crowns.

The English staked their claim on the vast expanse of land south of Canada along the eastern seaboard. The Dutch initially laid claim to areas that are now known as New Jersey and New York, but these were later ceded to the English crown in 1664.

The boundaries between what would become Canada and the United States were defined following the French and Indian War.

Meanwhile, Spanish territories, stretching from Florida across to the Louisiana Territory—a massive region covering much of today's Western and Midwestern United States—were transferred to American control in 1819 through purchase. Additionally, in 1867 what was termed as "Seward's Folly," the United States acquired Alaska from Russia for $7,000,000, further expanding its territory.

These historical transactions and territorial expansions underpinned the shaping of the modern United States, reflecting a period of intense exploration, conflict, and negotiation that eventually led to the establishment of its current borders.

Here's a quote from noted English Jurist Sir William Blackstone in 1765 regarding the ownership of land. The quote appears in Book II, Chapter I of Blackstone's magnum opus on English Common Law *Commentaries on the Laws of England*:

> "There is nothing which so generally engages the affections of mankind as the right of landed property. And yet there are few that will give themselves the trouble to consider the origin and foundation of this right. Pleased as we are with the possession, we seem afraid to look back to the means by which it was acquired, as if fearful of some defect in our title; or at best we rest, satisfied with the decision of the laws in our favor, without examining the reason or authority upon which those laws have been built. We think it enough that our title is derived by the grant of the former proprietor; not caring to reflect that *there is no foundation in nature or in natural law why a set of words upon parchment should convey the dominion of land.*"

4
AMERICAN TITLE RIGHTS STEM FROM GOVERNMENT

The naming of American colonial towns and regions—such as ElizabethTown, Charlestown, Jamestown, Williamsburg, Phillipsburg, Raleigh, Essex County, Baltimore, Pennsylvania and others—reflects the deep historical ties between these areas and the European monarchies, particularly the British Crown, that laid claim to them. These names serve as a testament to the period of European exploration, conquest, and colonization that reshaped the New World.

Initially, European powers acquired land through a combination of conquest, settlement, trade, and purchase, often celebrating their territorial gains and asserting their dominance by naming places after monarchs, influential figures, or places of origin.

As European influence expanded, the methods of acquiring land evolved—or devolved—into practices involving extortion and the imposition of treaties on Native American tribes. Many of these treaties, while purporting to be legal agreements, were often signed under duress or through deceptive practices, leading to the widespread dispossession of indigenous lands. Over time, these treaties, despite their dubious origins, served as the legal basis for European—and later American and Canadian—claims to the land, effectively sidelining Native American claims to their ancestral territories.

Regardless of the rights Native Americans might seem to hold within reservations, such as tax exemptions and the ability to run gambling casinos, these rights are contingent upon recognition by the authorities who transformed tribal lands into territories owned by European Crowns or the official governments of the United States or Canada. Essentially, the existence of Native American rights today hinges on the acknowledgment and concession of these governing bodies. Without such recognition, Native American rights would not be formally acknowledged.

Reconstruction Finance Corporation and Lucifer

How far back does title vesting go in modern America? Here's an interesting story to illustrate the issue in the context of title rights and government. In the 1930's a Louisiana attorney was attempting to obtain a government loan for a client. He'd researched land title back to 1803 thinking that was far enough back in time to claim a clear abstract of title. The loan was rejected. The bureaucrat wanted further proof of title before 1803.

In response the lawyer wrote this reply:

'Please be advised that in the year 1803, title to this land was vested in fee simple in the United States of America and the soundness of such title has never been before or since questioned. It is a matter of common knowledge in the state of Louisiana and may be of passing interest in Washington, District of Columbia, that in the year 1803, one Thomas Jefferson, then President of the United States and resident of Virginia, purchase for his principal, the United States of America, from one Napoleon Bonaparte, then Emperor of France, for and in consideration of the full sum of $27,267,622 or approximately four cents per acre, a vast territory commonly known as the 'Louisiana Purchase,' and including within its description the tract here under abstract.

'France acquired said property from Spain by virtue of a certain conquest and treaty. A copy of said treaty is not recorded in the records of this parish. The government of Spain acquired title on

October 12, 1492 by virtue of the discovery of one Christopher Columbus, traveler and explorer, a resident of Genoa, Italy, who by agreement concerning the acquisition of title to any land discovered, traveled and explored under the sponsorship and patronage of Her Majesty Isabella, Queen of Spain.'

'The good Queen, being a pious woman and careful about titles almost, I might say as the R.F.C. is, before she sold her jewels to help Columbus took the precaution of securing the sanction of her title by consent of the Pope, a resident of near Rome, Italy, and ex-officio personal representative on Earth of the Maker of the Earth. God made Louisiana along with the rest of the earth and can be assumed to be the original grantor.'

'My law clerk suggests that one Lucifer, whose residence is unknown to me, may have secured some prescriptive rights in Louisiana and other parts of the United States. If you think that his suggestion has merit, you are in a better position to secure a quit claim from the Devil than I. Trusting that this additional citation complies with your request and assuring you of our willingness to be of service, I am respectfully your servant.'

The Backstory — from England to America

Title vesting in modern America is a continuation of early English land ownership. It began in 1066 with the Norman Conquest by the Duke of Normandy, William.

As 'William the Conqueror' established the manorial or feudal land systems in England he had allotted land to his barons who were to render to him and to his successor certain services. These feudal services were in effect perpetual land rent to provide for the requirements of government.

In addition, areas of land were set aside for free use by the serfs as 'Commons' on which to grow food, pasture their domesticated animals, and cut firewood.

With an increasing population there is also more demand for wool. This pressured Barons to encroach upon the serf's Commons. By enclosing them for sheep pasture, the area of freeland allotted to the serfs was continually reduced.

A large part of the history of mankind is the story of population growth. This compelled the migration of people to acquire land on which to live and maintain themselves, and wars to govern. Conflicts were inevitable.

Mass migration of Europeans to America was caused not by a widespread desire for religious freedom, as has often been declared but, as shown here, by craving for land, and to escape the poverty in Europe emanating from feudalism.

Primogeniture and entail is a feudal concept to keep landed property from being broken up and descending to a female line. The law was designed to leave the bulk if not all of one's wealth to one heir, the eldest son. However, just like in the Roman fideicommissum, the use of a trust for holding title could circumvent these rules on succession.

Claims of land ownership is one of the most interesting subjects in American history because of settlements on the North American continent by five different European nations. And there were many naval and military fights between them. The significance of these land conflicts were historically important to the United States.

After the English conquest of other nationals, all the land in the English colonies in America was, by royal edict, claimed as the personal property of successive British monarchs, to do with as they please. The mere scratch of a goose quill in the hand of a European monarch given to his court favorites, their heir is assigned title to land and supported by armed force. The right to exact tribute of all who settled or were afterwards born in America, was without justification of any kind.

5
EVOLUTION OF TITLE LAW

Feudal Law — land ownership centralized under the authority of a king or emperor, then distributed to members of the nobility in exchange for military support or allegiance. Land further divided among lower-ranking vassals and serfs who worked the land, sharing its yield with their higher-ranking lords.

Common Law — is based upon the rulings and 'case law' of various courts at all levels throughout history.

Treaty Law — through which nations agree on boundary lines and borders which make real estate interests subservient to the particular country's laws in which the realty is situated.

Statute Law — which is enacted by various legislative bodies in the cities, counties, states, regions, and at federal level.

Realty Law — differentiates between general realty and personalty laws to create and recognize certain private property rights as well as such matters as

a. The Statute of Frauds, which requires real estate, conveyances, leases, sales contracts, option contracts and other instruments to be in writing.

b. Rules of devise and descent under which title passes directly to legal errors established by law or marriages or to beneficiaries by trust or to devisees by will.

c. Inchoate rights in real estate which were established by law, which include:

    1. Community Property Rights
    2. Dower Rights of Wives
    3. Curtesy Rights of Husbands

    All of which attach depending upon the applicable state law, at the time of marriage or, at the time the property is acquired after marriage.

d. Homestead Rights which protect title against certain kinds of creditors.

Evolution of Title

As society evolves we see many conflicts related to land ownership. Early on the resolution of those conflicts is often unclear and unjust. As a result there arises an understanding that title can include many circumstances and situations related to property ownership.

One simple example is what happens if the neighbor's cow tramples our crops? This animal destroys something of considerable value in agrarian society – a food supply. What relief is available for these damages?

Another example is farmers who work the land without actual ownership. What if the property owner needed to borrow money and wanted to use the land as collateral?

These practical situations led to a refinement and evolution of what 'title' actually means. Legal title alone was insufficient to address the circumstances. The concept of equitable title or interests began to solve many problems. Now let's address them in more detail.

6
LEGAL TITLE

Legal title is the term used for the rights of ownership that the law acknowledges over a specific property or asset. This concept confirms the legal right of an owner to use, control, and sell the property according to legal standards.

Whomever is listed on the deed is the legal title owner. They get their authority based upon real estate law.

Evidence of real property transactions must be in writing per the Statute of Frauds: a deed proves land ownership, a recorded mortgage shows a debt obligation. Bank statements or stock certificates represent financial assets. These documents, essential as they are, highlight how property and financial assets, while appearing physical and concrete, are fundamentally based on legal acknowledgment and paperwork. This emphasizes the importance of legal systems that validate these documents as

"Evidence of real property transactions must be in writing per the Statute of Frauds: a deed proves land ownership, a recorded mortgage shows a debt obligation."

proof of ownership, without which we would essentially own nothing.

In contrast, equitable title refers to having a beneficial interest in a property, where the actual legal title is held by someone else, such as in the arrangement of a trust. This distinction underlines the complexity of ownership and the crucial role of legal documentation in establishing and protecting our rights to property and assets.

"...equitable title refers to having a beneficial interest in a property, where the actual legal title is held by someone else, such as in the arrangement of a trust."

7
EQUITABLE TITLE

Equitable title is the right or beneficial interest a person holds in a property, despite not being the legal owner. While legal title denotes formal ownership as recognized by law, equitable title pertains to the benefits of using, possessing, and enjoying the property.

"While legal title denotes formal ownership as recognized by law, equitable title pertains to the benefits of using, possessing, and enjoying the property."

For instance, in a real estate transaction involving a loan, the lender, though not the legal owner, possesses equitable rights as loan security. Through specific agreements, these rights are granted in exchange for the loan. If the buyer fails to meet the loan conditions, the lender can claim legal ownership since the property serves as collateral.

Similarly, in a land contract, the buyer might hold equitable title, granting them the right to use and occupy the property based on the contract, even if the legal title remains with the seller or lender until contract conditions are met.

Equitable title embodies principles of fairness and justice, ensuring fair treatment for those with beneficial interests during transactions and legal processes. This concept, also known as bifurcation, separates the beneficial enjoyment of property from its legal ownership.

LEGAL TITLE	EQUITABLE TITLE
Property is formally recognized by law such as a deed.	Rights and/or Use of a Property without formal Ownership such as a Lease or Loan.

Table 1: Difference between Legal Title and Equitable Title

Created under equity law, which focuses on fairness over specific legal statutes, equitable title often arises from contracts, which can be explicit or implied by actions. An example is palimony, where courts have upheld agreements without written contracts. Understanding when and how equitable title is established helps owners better anticipate their rights and options. Even short-term leases may establish equitable title, depending on the agreement's nature and terms.

Typically, short-term leases don't affect equitable title significantly. However, long-term leases, especially those involving commercial properties or land that are leased for many years, present a different scenario. Such leases can effectively transfer substantial rights from the legal owner's fee simple estate to a tenant's equitable leasehold estate.

Eminent Domain

This refers to the power of the state. the United States Government is the ultimate 'legal title' owner of all land in

America. You may think you own a property but remain subservient to the law of eminent domain. Read USSC Kelo v. New London 2005.

Strategy Secrets

Let's talk for a moment about transfer taxes. These are automatically triggered when legal title to a property is transferred from a seller to a buyer.

Equity and tax courts also recognize that a leasehold interest can mirror a legal title transfer depending upon the lease duration. When a leasehold surpasses 30 years, including any renewal options, it may qualify for tax-free exchanges.

In certain states, the period needed to convert a lease from personal property to real property can be as short as 21 years where 'real estate' is defined in the relevant statutes as being any property held for at least one lifetime.

Additionally, properties leased for income production and held under long-term leases can benefit from depreciation tax treatments similar to those of outright ownership. If a leasehold with more than 30 years remaining is sold, any profit is subject to lower capital gains tax rates.

Long-term leases also offer a strategy for avoiding high transfer fees and escalating property taxes with each title transfer. Tax assessors often focus on deed transfers, potentially overlooking leases, which can offer tax advantages.

For high value real estate you can expect to pay a 12% stamp duty in London and 5.5% in Los Angeles. Foreigners pay 60% tax in Singapore and 7.5% in Hong Kong (see Table 2.) These surcharges only apply to legal title transfers. 99% of bureaucrats and investors focus on legal title transactions.

LOCATION	TRANSFER TAX
London	12%
Los Angeles, California	5.5%
Singapore	60%
Hong Kong	7.5%

Table 2: Taxes on high value real estate property in different locations

Utilizing leases, whether they include options or not, along with determinable fee simple estates, can serve as a method to bypass transfer taxes. Furthermore, this approach keeps your name out of public records.

One investor secured a 99-year lease on a piece of land. Initially, this arrangement won't incur any property income taxes and is likely to stay under the radar, despite the property's value significantly increasing over the lease term compared to its current valuation on property tax documents. Additionally, for the next 69 years, this lease qualifies as a like-kind exchange under IRC section 1031, allowing for tax-deferred exchanges. Alternatively, the lease could be liquidated at a more opportune moment, such as when tax rates are lower.

Short-term leases can also establish equitable title, especially when they include a purchase option. This situation often poses challenges for small landlords. The specific details and context of each lease/option agreement play a crucial role in its legal interpretation. If the contract clearly provides an economic benefit to the optionee (the individual holding the option) for completing the purchase, an equitable title interest is established.

If the tenant/optionee fails to fulfill the lease terms, simply evicting them doesn't legally remove their equitable rights. Instead, a judicial foreclosure of the lease/option is required, unless the contract specifies a different procedure.

The presence of an equitable title interest in lease options typically depends on the financial benefit to the optionee. Criteria for this include any lease that allows payments to significantly count towards the purchase price or down payment, or offers rent below the market rate, thereby granting equitable title.

If you're the tenant/optionee you want the lease with option in a single document.

If you're the landlord/optionor you want the lease and option in two separate documents. (See Image 1.)

Another approach to safeguard the equity in your property, whether you own it outright or have a minimal mortgage, involves leveraging financial tools. For instance, an investor obtained a line of credit secured by a blanket mortgage across his entire portfolio of rental properties. This strategy immediately safeguarded millions in assets and years of accumulated wealth.

As you can now see, equitable title is powerful. Learn how to use it wisely.

RECORDING REQUESTED BY

AND WHEN RECORDED MAIL TO:

Name

Street
Address

City &
State
Zip

Title Order No. Escrow No.

SPACE ABOVE THIS LINE FOR RECORDER'S USE

Memorandum of Option

Assessor Parcel Number: ____________________

THIS MEMORANDUM OF OPTION TO PURCHASE is made and entered into on ____________________ by and between ____, "Optionor" and ____, "Optionee."

Optionor hereby grants to Optionee an Option to purchase for a term of ____________________, commencing on ________________ and ending on ________________, on the terms and conditions set forth in the Option by and between the parties hereto dated ________________, all the terms and conditions of which are made a part of this Memorandum of Option as though fully set forth herein, the premises in the County of ________________, State of California, described as follows:

EXECUTED ON ____________________

> A notary public or other officer completing this certificate verifies only the identity of the individual who signed the document to which this certificate is attached, and not the truthfulness, accuracy, or validity of that document.

STATE OF CALIFORNIA
COUNTY OF ____________________

On ______________________________ before me,

____
(here insert name and title of the officer)

,notary public, personally appeared ____________________

______________________________,

who proved to me on the basis of satisfactory evidence to be the person(s) whose name(s) is/are subscribed to the within instrument and acknowledged to me that he/she/they executed the same in his/her/their authorized capacity(ies), and that by his/her/their signature(s) on the instrument the person(s), or the entity upon behalf of which the person(s) acted, executed the instrument.

I certify under PENALTY OF PERJURY under the laws of the state of California that the foregoing paragraph is true and correct.

WITNESS my hand and official seal

Signature ______________________________

____
OPTIONOR

____
OPTIONOR

____
OPTIONEE

____
OPTIONEE

(This area for official notarial seal)

Image 1: Option Memorandum

8
ESTATES

Because it's possible to hold a variety of degrees of interest in land, real estate law defines these interests into various classifications.

They're only three basic major subdivisions of real estate interest. Referred to as 'estates,' these classifications include:

- Quantity of Interest
- Time of Enjoyment
- Number and connection of owners

Quantity of interest is further subdivided into freehold and non-freehold estates. The difference between free and non-free is 'time' of duration.

Freehold Estates — fee simple, fee defeasible, life, and other qualified estates.

Fee simple estate ownership, also called fee simple absolute, is the

> "Fee simple estate ownership, also called fee simple absolute, is the largest and most prevalent interest in land representing complete ownership."

largest and most prevalent interest in land representing complete ownership. It entitles the title holder to use or not to use the land in any way he or she sees fit, subject to the powers of the state to limit, control or condemn it both during the owner's lifetime and afterwards, as part of his or her estate planning. It can be created by will (devise) or descent or through force of law in the absence of a will (probate).

If real estate consists of a bundle of rights then fee simple title consists of the largest possible bundle of these rights that could be made available. It's the ownership standard against which all other interests and real estate must be held in terms of quantity of rights owned and/or the time of holding. Conveyance of a fee simple estate by a deed of conveyance from a competent grantor is the most common type of real estate transaction in the United States today. It's probably how you own your own residence.

Fee simple estates are generally thought of as being perpetual in that they can be passed from one generation to the next by will without ever being sold. One estate in England called Spain's Hall was originally a feudal grant. It had been in the same family since the 12th century.

Fee simple defeasible has specific conditions placed upon a buyer. If they fail to perform an act or violate restrictions, then the property can revert to the seller.

When an estate is held only for the lifetime of the title holder, it's called a life estate. These freehold estates are of indefinite duration which continue until a particular event after which time title to the property automatically reverts to another party. During the period prior to this reversion, they may not sell, gift, or devise the property.

The triggering reversionary event can be the death of either the holder of the fee simple estate or of a totally unrelated party or last to die of several parties.

The ultimate title holder possesses what was once termed a fee tail estate but which is now called a remainder estate.

Non-Freehold Estates — Estates for Years, Estates from Year to Year, Estates at Will, and estates at sufferance.

Also called 'leasehold estates' because they are less than a lifetime.

Estates for Years have a definite beginning and ending date. There is no minimum nor maximum time frame.

Estates from Year to Year are also known as periodic tenancy. This can be a weekly, monthly or annual term between the property owner and a tenant.

Estates at Will have no set guidelines. Either party may give notice to vacate at anytime. This is how innkeepers and hotels operate.

Life Estates and Estates for Years are often used for charitable trusts. They are either 'lead or remainder' and can be useful for asset protection.

Property is contributed to a charitable lead trust. For the life of the donor the charity gets the income. Upon death the property reverts to an heir.

Property is contributed to a charitable remainder trust. For the life of the donor you, spouse, et al gets the income. Upon death the property reverts to specific charity.

NOTE: Judgment liens against holders of a life estate or estate for years will not attach to their real property interests. This is because they'll automatically extinguish at a future date. Liens only attach to present interests, not future.

Remaindermen Strategies

A life estate and remainder estate is created—by a grant from one party or parties to another party or parties.

In the case of a life estate, the estate ends at the death of the grantor. The remainder estate terminates and automatically converts into a fee simple estate.

Optionally, a subsequent remainder estate is created by either the original grantor or the holder of the remainder estate.

Remainder estates can be subdivided among several remaindermen in a single generation or in a sequence of remaindermen, one following the lifetime of another for generations. This can provide interesting estate planning tools when combined with other estates and trust strategies.

Remainder rights are passed automatically without the need to file or execute any other instrument in the public records. However this requires the remainder rights and Remainderman were identified in the previously recorded conveyance to succeed a preceding life estate, or estate for years subject to the same limitations, restrictions, and vulnerabilities that may have been present in the prior estate.

Prior life or estate for years holders are accountable to the remainder estate holders and can be held liable for any waste or deterioration to the property during their tenure.

In rare instances where blatant neglect and abuse has been evident, courts have caused life or estate for years forfeited to remainder estate holders prior to the time than they would have normally been passed to them. Whether caused by courts or the passage of time, the entity to whom an estate passes is called one of the following:

A 'vested remainderman' if his/her/its identity is known.

A 'remainderman' if his/her/its specific identity is unknown.

This story carries an important lesson: being positioned as a remainderman behind a seemingly harmless holder of an estate for years can serve as a powerful strategy for protecting assets, one that's challenging to contest under any conditions.

This tactic relies on the principle of title law, which stipulates that liens can only attach to current interests. When both the estate for years and the remainder interest are encumbered by existing liens, it creates a complex situation that only the most determined individuals would dare to tackle.

For asset protection or bankruptcy one rarely known powerful technique is the use of a 'contingent remainderman.' These are also known as options. You do not presently hold legal title. It is conditioned upon a future event which may or may not occur. This is another secret strategy that can blindside your opponents at the last minute.

9
ESCROW PROCESS

Often when buying a property a neutral third-party escrow company will handle all the paperwork including loan docs and prepare the deeds for recording.

During this process you will be asked how to fill out a single page document, 'statement of information,' (SOI) to confirm your identity. (See Images 2a and 2b.)

The SOI is obtained from both the seller and buyer. It includes full names, SSN, DOB, marital status, and previous addresses. This data is necessary for positive identification of all individuals. It also helps distinguish parties in the transaction from others who may have similar names. This is to provide buyers 'clear' title and prevent fraud.

As a buyer you will get asked how do you want to hold title?

Your options include sole ownership, joint ownership, marital property, a trust, or a business organization, etc. This is what anyone will see on the recorded deed which is public info.

If you request advice from the escrow officer, they might give you a brochure or an information sheet outlining your choices. They possess knowledge about the technical processes involved in different ways of holding title and can discuss these intelligently. However, they will refrain from offering legal advice.

STATEMENT OF INFORMATION
CONFIDENTIAL INFORMATION FOR YOUR PROTECTION

Completion of this statement expedites your application for title insurance, as it assists in establishing identity, eliminating matters affecting persons with similar names and avoiding the use of fraudulent or forged documents. Complete all blanks (please print) or indicate "none" or "N/A." If more space is needed for any item(s), use the reverse side of the form. Each party (and spouse/domestic partner, if applicable) to the transaction should personally sign this form.

ESCROW NO.: ______________ TITLE NO.: ______________

NAME AND PERSONAL INFORMATION

First Name ______ Middle/Maiden name *(If none, indicate)* ______ Last Name ______

Home Phone: ______ Business Phone: ______ Date of Birth: ______

Birthplace: ______ Social Security No.: ______ Driver's License No.: ______

List any other name you have used or been known by: ______

State of residence: ______ I have lived continuously in the U.S.A. since ______

Are you currently married? ______ If yes, complete the following information:

Date and place of marriage: ______

Spouse: First Name ______ Middle/Maiden name *(If none, indicate)* ______ Last Name ______

Business Phone: ______ Date of Birth: ______ Birthplace: ______

Social Security No.: ______ Driver's License No.: ______

Are you currently a registered domestic partner? ______ If yes, complete the following information:

Domestic Partner: First Name ______ Middle/Maiden name *(If none, indicate)* ______ Last Name ______

Home Phone: ______ Business Phone: ______ Date of Birth: ______

Birthplace: ______ Social Security No.: ______ Driver's License No.: ______

List any other name you have used or been known by: ______

State of residence: ______ I have lived continuously in the U.S.A. since ______

RESIDENCES (LAST 10 YEARS)

Number & Street ______ City ______ From (date) to (date) ______

Number & Street ______ City ______ From (date) to (date) ______

(If more space is required, use reverse side of form)

OCCUPATIONS/BUSINESSES (LAST 10 YEARS)

______

Image 2a: Statement of Information

Firm or Business name — Address — From (date) to (date)

Firm or Business name — Address — From (date) to (date)

(If more space is required, use reverse side of form)

SPOUSE'S/DOMESTIC PARTNER'S OCCUPATIONS/BUSINESSES (LAST 10 YEARS)

Firm or Business name — Address — From (date) to (date)

Firm or Business name — Address — From (date) to (date)

(If more space is required, use reverse side of form)

PRIOR MARRIAGE(S)

Any prior marriages for either spouse? ________ If yes, complete the following:
Prior spouse's name: ________ Prior Spouse of Husband: ________
Marriage terminated by: Death ____ Divorce ____ Date of termination: ________

Prior spouse's name: ________ Prior Spouse of Husband: ________
Marriage terminated by: Death ____ Divorce ____ Date of termination: ________

(If more space is required, use reverse side of form)

PRIOR DOMESTIC PARTNERSHIP(S)

Any prior domestic partnerships for either person? ________ If yes, complete the following:
Prior partner's name: ________ Prior Partner: ________
Partnership terminated by: Death ____ Dissolution ____ Nullification ____ Termination ____
Date of termination: ________

Prior partner's name: ________ Prior Partner: ________
Partnership terminated by: Death ____ Dissolution ____ Nullification ____ Termination ____
Date of termination: ________

(If more space is required, use reverse side of form)

INFORMATION ABOUT THE PROPERTY

Buyer intends to reside on the property in this transaction: Yes ________ No ________

OWNER TO COMPLETE THE FOLLOWING ITEMS

Street Address of Property in this transaction: ________
The land is unimproved ________; or improved with a structure of the following type:
A Single or 1-4 Family ________ Condo Unit ________ Other ________

Image 2b: Statement of Information

This caution is due to the significant impact that the choice of title-holding method can have on your finances, estate planning, and legal rights. At this point, they will suggest consulting with a real estate attorney or seeking guidance from independent resources.

Title insurance described later in this book is generally connected to the escrow process.

10
VESTING TITLE — REAL PROPERTY

Your legal title vesting method is described on the grant or warranty deed. This is essentially a bill of sale that demonstrates to the world that a seller has sold their property to a buyer.

- Seller is the Grantor.
- Buyer is the Grantee.

In many legal instruments 'or' is the giver and 'ee' is the recipient.

On this deed you will see the new legal owner. Your choice of single or joint ownership, a trust, or business organization is the grantee.

For a title transfer to be valid, it's not mandatory for the deed to be recorded or notarized. However, both delivery and acceptance by the involved parties are essential. Essentially, a transfer cannot occur without the recipient agreeing to accept what is being offered.

But typically, deeds are notarized and officially recorded. This process serves as constructive notice, informing everyone that the legal title to a property has changed hands. Before the era of written deeds, property transfers were announced orally during Sunday church services to ensure the community was aware of the ownership change.

County Recorder

The purpose of any county recorder's office is to provide an informational database of public records. These records are also known as 'constructive notice' of transactions related to real estate such as grant deeds.

> "Before the era of written deeds, property transfers were announced orally during Sunday church services to ensure the community was aware of the ownership change."

They also keep birth, marriage, divorce and death records. Civil marriage ceremonies are performed. Notary registrations and bonds are recorded too. However, they are not a governmental body themselves, only a keeper of public records.

Originally all records were kept in heavy cloth bound paper books. This meant you had to physically go to the recorder's office to search any record. It was tedious. But now they're online. This makes it easy for anyone to look up basic records. But there is a big difference between data found on their external website versus their in-house system.

Now let's explore the different forms of vesting.

Sole Ownership

One person owns all rights, title, and interest. They have unilateral decision-making authority regarding the property. They can decide how the property is used, who can live there, whether to lease it out, make improvements, sell it, or pass it on to heirs.

Listed below are several common vesting cases of sole ownership by an individual person. This language will be included on your deed.

A 'single man/woman' refers to a man who has never been married. For example, "John Smith, a single man."

An 'unmarried man/woman' refers to a woman who was previously married and is now legally divorced. For example, "Katherine Staedtler, an unmarried woman."

A 'married man/woman' as his/her Sole and Separate property. This is a man or woman who acquires title in his/her name alone. For example, "Jose Martinez, a married man, as his sole and separate property."

Joint Tenants with Rights of Survivorship — JTWROS

Joint tenancy is a form of co-ownership where two or more individuals hold an equal interest in a property simultaneously, with rights of survivorship. This means that upon the death of one joint tenant, their interest in the property automatically passes to the surviving joint tenant(s), regardless of what may be stated in a will.

While joint tenancy is a popular choice among married couples due to its right of survivorship feature, it is not limited to married partners. Unmarried partners, family members, friends, or business partners can also hold property as joint tenants, provided they meet the criteria of joint tenancy.

The requirements for joint tenancy include these four unities:

1. Unity of Possession: All joint tenants have equal rights to occupy and use all parts of the property. Unlike other forms of ownership, there is no specific allocation of portions for each joint tenant.

2. Unity of Interest: All joint tenants hold an equal ownership interest in the property. Each has an undivided interest in the entire property. For example, if there are two joint tenants, each owns 50% of the property. If there are three, each owns 33.3% of the property.

3. Unity of Time: All joint tenants acquire their interest at the same time.

4. Unity of Title: All joint tenants acquire their interest under the same deed or conveyance act.

Here are three variations of joint tenants vesting:

- John Buyer and Jill Buyer, husband and wife as joint tenants with rights of survivorship.

- John Buyer a single man and Jill Buyer, an unmarried woman as joint tenants with rights of survivorship.

- John Buyer, a married man as his sole and separate property, and Jill Buyer, a single woman, and ABC Trust with JD as Trustee, as joint tenants with rights of survivorship.

However, if any of the joint tenants were to subsequently sell or give away their interest before death, then ownership converts from joint tenants to tenants in common. Few are aware of this consequence.

Community Property without Rights of Survivorship

A form of vesting title to property owned by husband and wife during their marriage (and in select places, registered domestic partners) which they intend to own together.

Community property is distinguished from separate property, which is property acquired before marriage, by separate gift or bequest, after legal separation, or which is agreed in writing to be owned by one spouse.

In California, real property conveyed to a married man or woman is presumed to be community property, unless otherwise stated. Since all such property is owned equally, husband and wife must sign all agreements and documents transferring the property or using it as security for a loan.

Under community property, each spouse has the right to dispose of one half of the community property, by will.

For example, "John Buyer and Jill Buyer, husband and wife as community property."

Community Property *with* Rights of Survivorship

This form of holding title has many of the characteristics of Community Property but adds the benefit of the right of survivorship

There may be tax benefits for holding title in this manner. Since 2003 California has recognized this form of vesting for both married couples and domestic partners.

John Buyer and Jill Buyer, husband and wife, as community property with right of survivorship.

Jose Martinez and Karen Harewood, registered domestic partners, as community property with rights of survivorship.

Martha Thomas and Sarah Moreau, registered domestic partners, as community property with rights of survivorship.

Note that community property vesting is only recognized in 9 states — Arizona, California, Idaho, Louisiana, New Mexico, Texas, Washington, Wisconsin.

Upon the death of a spouse/partner, the decedent's interest ends and the surviving spouse/partner owns the property by survivorship and now in severalty. The survivor owns 100%. Other factors include a step up in tax basis.

Unless there is a prenup, state laws dictate who gets what in the event of divorce. Couples with complex estates or blended families may prefer other vesting formats such as multiple living trusts.

Interspousal Transfers

An interspousal transfer deed is a legal instrument often used in community property states to transfer ownership of real property between married spouses.

This type of deed is commonly utilized in the context of marriage dissolution (divorce), estate planning, or in the refinancing of a property to clearly define property ownership rights between spouses.

Interspousal deeds are particularly useful for transferring property without the typical sale and purchase process. They generally avoid property tax reassessment and are exempt from documentary transfer taxes.

Other benefits of interspousal transfers can include simplified estate planning for blended families or complex estates.

Tenants in Common — TIC

Tenancy in common is another form of legal title ownership where two or more individuals hold an undivided fractional interest in a specific property— residential or commercial.

Unlike joint tenancy, tenants in common do not have the right of survivorship. Instead, each tenant in common can individually sell, transfer, or bequeath at death their share of the property to another party.

They may also mortgage their individual interest in the property without the consent of the other co-tenants.

Their interests may be equal or unequal, in quantity or duration. Ownership periods may occur at different times. All have an equal right to possess and use the entire property, regardless of the size of their individual ownership interests.

Everyone is entitled to a portion of the income and responsible for property upkeep, maintenance and taxes based upon their percentage share.

The specific amount of ownership is established by inserting in the deed vesting the percentage of interest that each of the buyers will hold. Here's an example:

Mary S. Jones, a single woman, as to an undivided 3/4 interest and John Q. Brown, an unmarried man, as to the remaining undivided 1/4 interest as tenants in common.

Cathy C. Carrot, a single woman, as to an undivided 2/3 interest and Northwest LLC a Utah Company, as to the remaining undivided 1/3 interest as tenants in common.

If no percentage is set-forth, each tenant is presumed to own an equal percentage.

Corporations

Due to the income tax classification of Corporations (Sub C) they are unsuitable for owning real estate. Penalties include double taxation and inability to transact 1031 exchanges. There is no step up in basis after death.

Limited Liability Company — LLC

These business organizations are popular with real estate investors for holding legal title. The grant or warranty deed will list the LLC itself as grantee owner.

Based upon permission from and compliance with the Secretary of State, LLC members are afforded limited liability. This means that the personal assets of the members are generally protected from the business debts and liabilities of the LLC.

However, sole member (vs multi-member) LLCs are at risk of tax audit. Creditors may pierce the veil resulting in attachment of personal assets. Court rulings are inconsistent. Few are aware of this fact.

For Example: Intermountain Investments LLC, a Colorado Company.

Members can gift or sell their shares without changing legal title. LLCs must now disclose personal details of controlling shareholders per the Corporate Transparency Act.

Trust Vesting

These are arrangements whereby legal title to property is transferred from a grantor to a trustee(s). Depending upon the type of trust, a trustee has different responsibilities and authorizations. The trustee always acts as a fiduciary on behalf of the beneficiaries.

Living Trust

This type of personal trust is designed for estate planning.

It holds personal and business assets that are later distributed in an estate. By default they are initially revocable, becoming irrevocable after death. Living Trusts are often used to bypass probate proceedings.

Legal title to real estate lists the trustee on the deed.

For example: Giovanni Bruno as Trustee, of the Bruno Family Trust DTD 01/01/2023.

Living Trusts are ideal for title to a personal residence. There is no privacy, nor asset protection. The biggest benefit is avoiding probate and to quietly distribute an estate.

Land Trust

The modern day purpose of a land trust is privacy for the beneficiaries. And this trust operates the opposite than others.

Trustee(s) holds legal and equitable title. They execute deeds, mortgages, leases, and otherwise deal with the property. Unlike with other trusts, in this case, they do not make decisions. They are passive and only act upon the written direction of the beneficiaries.

Rent collection, improvements, and property management is controlled by the beneficiaries. They exercise all rights of ownership without holding legal title.

The Massachusetts Business Trust migrated to Illinois in 1892 when Chicago Title Company formed what is now called the 'Illinois Type Land Trust.' Its original purpose was to effect partial releases for a loan encumbering a large tract of land with a subdivision tract.

It remains a common law trust and benefits from thousands of case histories.

In these types of trusts the trustee could be a natural person such as with the living trust or an institutional trustee such as a bank or trust company. Examples:

- A. Green as Trustee of the Midwestern Community Trust DTD 01/01/2023.

- Security Trust Company as Trustee of the Procell #867 Investment Trust DTD 01/01/2023.

The biggest benefit is privacy for the beneficiary(ies) if the deed is prepared correctly. There is no asset protection, limited liability nor tax benefits with a land trust.

Business Trust

This commercial trust is designed to operate a for profit business run by an active trustee(s). It offers asset protection, bankruptcy provision, and income tax options.

Although a business organization, it can operate with or without permission from the Secretary of State. It's ideal for investment real estate with a single or multiple investors.

Legal title vesting of the grantee reads similar to other trusts – for example:

- Simon Moreaux as Trustee for the Mercosur Trading Trust DTD 01/01/2023.

- Aerostream Inc, a Wyoming Corporation as Trustee for the Hilti Management Company DTD 01/01/2023.

Just like with a Land Trust the deed must be prepared correctly. A standard deed only provides partial anonymity. Few are aware of this fact. My recommendation is to learn how to fill out the deed correctly in order to preserve your anonymity and protect your assets.

RECORDING REQUESTED BY

AND WHEN RECORDED MAIL THIS DEED AND, UNLESS OTHERWISE SHOWN BELOW, MAIL TAX STATEMENT TO:

Name

Street Address

City & State Zip

Title Order No. Escrow No.

SPACE ABOVE THIS LINE FOR RECORDER'S USE

Grant Deed

THE UNDERSIGNED GRANTOR (S) DECLARE (S) APN: ____________

DOCUMENTARY TRANSFER TAX IS $ ____________

☐ unincorporated area City of ____________

☐ computed on full value of interest or property conveyed, or
☐ computed on full value less value of liens or encumbrances remaining at time of sale, and

FOR A VALUABLE CONSIDERATION, receipt of which is hereby acknowledged,

hereby GRANT(S) to

the following described real property in the

County of , state of California

Dated

A notary public or other officer completing this certificate verifies only the identity of the individual who signed the document to which this certificate is attached, and not the truthfulness, accuracy, or validity of that document.

STATE OF CALIFORNIA
COUNTY OF ____________

On ____________ before me,

____
(here insert name and title of the officer)

,notary public, personally appeared ____________

____________,
who proved to me on the basis of satisfactory evidence to be the person(s) whose name(s) is/are subscribed to the within instrument and acknowledged to me that he/she/they executed the same in his/her/their authorized capacity(ies), and that by his/her/their signature(s) on the instrument the person(s), or the entity upon behalf of which the person(s) acted, executed the instrument.

I certify under PENALTY OF PERJURY under the laws of the state of California that the foregoing paragraph is true and correct.

WITNESS my hand and official seal

Signature ____________ (This area for official notarial seal)

MAIL TAX STATEMENTS TO PARTY SHOWN ON FOLLOWING LINE; IF NO PARTY SHOWN, MAIL AS DIRECTED ABOVE

Name Street Address City, State & Zip

Image 3: Grant Deed

11
LEGAL PROCEEDINGS

Anytime real estate is placed into a corporation or trust that's domiciled in another legal jurisdiction, any legal matters concerning the property 'legal title' owner must be addressed in the jurisdiction of the corporation or trust — not where the property is situated. This strategy has been used by owners of high-risk properties for years, placing them in trusts in another state to circumvent issues.

Transferring real estate into a trust often changes the nature of the ownership from real property to personal property. This not only allows for the selection of more favorable legal venues but also means that any judgment liens arising would not attach to the personal property interests, such as those represented by shares in the trust.

> "Transferring real estate into a trust often changes the nature of the ownership from real property to personal property."

But know that even if the court can't attack or attach the vested owner holding legal title, they can place an equitable judgment lien against the property in the county it's located.

In legal disputes, the party involved could be an individual, a married couple, an LLC Manager, or a Trust Trustee. It's important to consult the deed to ensure the correct entity is named.

"...even if the court can't attack or attach the vested owner holding legal title, they can place an equitable judgment lien against the property in the county it's located."

Personal Notes on Vesting

When I first started investing in real estate, LLCs were the standard go to. All the lawyers and real estate clubs advocated them. But in 1995 I discovered land trusts from one super smart guy, Jack Miller. I quickly discarded LLCs. A much better solution is a Trust.

Compared to LLCs the Land Trusts were so much easier and quicker to set up. They also offered many hidden advantages. In dozens and dozens of real property transactions I personally used and advocated to clients to use land trusts for title.

They enabled us to avoid property tax reassessments. And today you can use them to avoid stamp duties or transfer taxes.

Years later we shifted to business trusts for better safety and income tax options. I made a video to explain the benefits.

Now we'll shift to a discussion about liens. The simplest lien example is a real estate purchase contract. Once a buyer and seller have agreed upon a deal their signed contract effectively becomes a lien against the property.

12
LIENS ON REAL ESTATE

Liens come into being as a security for a voluntary promise.

Promise obligations can include debt, leases, options, alimony, construction, purchase contracts, etc. But a promise itself without specific security doesn't create the lien.

You create the lien by 'securitizing' the real estate as collateral. There are typically two written documents (See Images 4 and 5.) One is the promise (note, lease, option, etc.) agreement. Second is the security instrument (mortgage, deed of trust). This creates an 'equitable' title interest for the lienholder.

"Liens generally impact the ability to sell or transfer 'legal' title until the underlying promise obligation is satisfied."

—*We can also use a standard trust instrument parallel — beneficiaries hold an equitable interest while trustees hold legal title.*

Liens generally impact the ability to sell or transfer 'legal' title until the underlying promise obligation is satisfied. However, legal title can transfer with the lien obligation passing to the next person. It's often called "subject to" an existing obligation.

Liens are 'perfected' by recording the security instrument (mortgage or deed of trust) with the County Recorder's office.

Leases, options, loan agreements can be recorded separately or within the security instrument. These are public documents for anyone to search and inspect.

Title Theory vs Lien Theory

When real estate is used for security for a promise to pay (loan), the paperwork is different depending upon whether the transaction is in—a lien theory or title theory state.

Lien Theory—Mortgage. In eastern states when a property is financed through a mortgage loan, the lender places a mortgage lien on the property. The borrower retains both legal and equitable title. This specific lien serves as security for the loan which creates a 'conditional estate.' It allows the lender to judicially foreclose on the property if the borrower defaults on the mortgage payments. These are 'two-party' arrangements in which the buyer retains both legal and equitable title.

After the loan is paid off, the mortgage lien is released by filing a 'Satisfaction' in the public record.

Title Theory—Deed of Trust. In western states when a property is financed with a trust deed loan, a trust is actually created. The borrower is the trustor. A third party holding legal title is trustee. The lender holding an equitable title interest is the beneficiary. This lien serves as security for the loan, allowing the lender to non-judicially foreclose on the property if the borrower defaults on the loan payments. These are 'three-party' arrangements in which the buyer makes a conveyance of legal title to the trustee.

After the loan is satisfied, legal title is then transferred back to the now 'paid off' borrower trustor. The lender's equitable interest ceases to exist and is recaptured by the borrower.

In either case the lender of a defaulted loan may force an auction to recover the loan balance plus fees, etc. A successful sale will apply the proceeds to the unpaid debt with any excess balance going to junior creditors or the borrower.

Defaulted lenders can bypass the power sale under the Deed of Trust and sue the trustor on the promise to pay. This is a deficiency option. It creates a judgment lien which then attaches to the defaulting borrower's property, wages, bank accounts, home furnishings, cars, RV's, etc.

One Action Rule—this CA law means that a lender must first liquidate the secured real estate before pursuing a borrower's other assets.

Generally there is no personal liability on the borrower for unpaid debts under a deed of trust. Only the property itself is at risk. These are also called non-recourse loans.

RECORDING REQUESTED BY:

When Recorded Mail Document To:

APN:

SPACE ABOVE THIS LINE FOR RECORDER'S USE

SHORT FORM DEED OF TRUST AND ASSIGNMENT OF RENTS

THIS DEED OF TRUST, made ____________________, between ______________________________, herein called **TRUSTOR,** whose address is ______________________________,

______________________________, herein called **TRUSTEE,** and

______________________________, herein called **BENEFICIARY,**

WITNESSETH: That Trustor IRREVOCABLY GRANTS, TRANSFERS AND ASSIGNS to TRUSTEE IN TRUST, WITH POWER OF SALE, that property in ______________________ County, ______________________, California described as:

See Exhibit A attached hereto and made a part hereof.

TOGETHER WITH the rents, issues and profits thereof, SUBJECT, HOWEVER, to the right, power and authority given to and conferred upon Beneficiary by paragraph (10) of the provisions incorporated herein by reference to collect and apply such rents, issues and profits.

For the Purpose of Securing:

1. Performance of each agreement of Trustor incorporated by reference or contained herein.
2. Payment of the indebtedness evidenced by one Promissory Note of even date herewith, and any extension or renewal thereof, in the principal sum of **$**______________________ executed by Trustor in favor of Beneficiary or order.
3. Payment of such further sums as the then record owner of said property hereafter may borrow from Beneficiary, when evidenced by another note (or notes) reciting it is so secured.

INITIALS: _____ _____ _____ _____

SHORT FORM DEED OF TRUST

Image 4: Deed of Trust

DO NOT DESTROY THIS NOTE: When paid, this note, with Deed of Trust securing same, must be surrendered to Trustee for cancellation before reconveyance will be made.

NOTE SECURED BY DEED OF TRUST

(INSTALLMENT – INTEREST INCLUDED)

$ ____________________, California ____________________

In installments as herein stated, for value received, I promise to pay to ______________________________ or order at ______________________________ the principal sum of ______________________________ dollars with interest from __________ on unpaid principal at the rate of __________ per cent per annum; principal and interest payable in installments of ______________________________ dollars or more on the __________ day of each __________ month, beginning on the __________ day of __________ and continuing until ______________________________

Each payment shall be credited first on interest then due; and the remainder on principal, and the interest shall thereupon cease upon the principal so credited. Should default be made in payment of any installment of principal and interest, the whole sum of principal and interest shall, at the option of the holder of this note, become immediately due. Principal and interest payable in lawful money of the United States. If action be instituted on this note; the undersigned promise(s) to pay such sum as the Court may adjudge as attorney's fees. This note is secured by a DEED OF TRUST to **CHICAGO TITLE COMPANY, a California corporation, as Trustee.**

THIS FORM FURNISHED BY CHICAGO TITLE

Image 5: Promissory Note

A Full Reconveyance will be issued only when the original Note or Notes, together with the Deed of Trust securing payment thereof, are surrendered to the Trustee for cancellation, accompanied by this Request signed by all owners of the Note or Notes, together with the required fees.

REQUEST FOR FULL RECONVEYANCE

TO ______________________________, TRUSTEE

The undersigned is the legal owner and holder of the Note or Notes for the original sum of $________________ , and of all other indebtedness secured by Deed of Trust dated ______________ made by ____, Trustor, to ______________________________ Trustee, and recorded on _________, as instrument number ______________ in Book ______ , Page _________, of Official Records, in the office of the County Recorder of ______________________, California.

Said Note or Notes, together will all other indebtedness secured by said Deed of Trust, have been fully paid and satisfied; and you are hereby requested and directed, upon delivery to you of said Deed of Trust and said Note or Notes and upon payment to you of any sums owing to you under the terms of said Deed of Trust, to cancel said Note or Notes above mentioned, and all other evidences of indebtedness secured by said Deed of Trust, together with the said Deed of Trust, and to reconvey, without warranty, to the parties legally entitled thereto, all the estate now held by you under the Deed of Trust.

Dated: ____________________________

____

Mail Reconveyance to ____

Image 6: Request for Full Reconveyance

Other Types of Real Estate Liens

Mechanic's Liens: Contractors, subcontractors, or suppliers who provide labor or materials for construction or improvements on a property may file mechanic's liens to secure payment for their services. These liens provide a legal claim on the property until the debt is satisfied.

Liens can also be imposed by law without the knowledge of the property owner. This includes various types of statutory liens, such as mechanics and materialmen's liens. These liens apply specifically to improvements made on the property, not to the land itself, and are enacted based on the property owner's requests under different state laws, known as 'contract statutes' or 'consent statutes.'

If a property owner agrees to work and then fails to pay for it, a lien can be placed on the property. However, if a tenant initiates the work, the situation may differ. If the owner does not object and benefits from the improvements—either through a satisfied tenant or increased property rentability—consent statutes come into play, and a lien may still be attached, regardless of who ordered the work and whether there is a written contract. This is governed by the 'doctrine of equity.' In most jurisdictions, such liens need to be enforced within a specific timeframe; otherwise, they expire due to the Statute of Limitations.

In Pennsylvania, property owners can find themselves liable for a mechanic's lien placed by subcontractors who have not received payment from their contractor, even if the owner has paid the contractor in full. These liens are referred to as specific statutory liens. To avoid this situation, it is advisable for owners to either issue checks jointly to both the contractor and subcontractor, or to utilize an escrow account to manage payments.

Property Tax Liens: If a property owner does not pay their property taxes, local governments can impose tax liens on the property. These liens grant the government a legal claim over the property, which can lead to a tax sale or foreclosure if the outstanding taxes are not settled.

This tax obligation always takes priority on a property's title, which is why lenders place great importance on borrowers keeping up with property tax payments. To ensure these taxes are paid, lenders often set up impound accounts that collect property taxes as part of the monthly mortgage payments. Even though a lender's lien might technically hold the 'first' position, property taxes will always have precedence.

Income Tax Liens: At the federal level the IRS sells liens, partial releases of liens, and foreclosed liens. They are sold for cash and often at discounts.

Consider a scenario where a property is seized for unpaid taxes and has an existing mortgage lien (See Image 7.) If the IRS lien ranks after the mortgage in priority and the borrower's payments cease, the lending company can initiate foreclosure. The IRS then has 120 days to repay the mortgage balance in full to reclaim the property. However, without a budget for these defaulted loans, and if this property is the taxpayer's only collateral, it's unlikely that the IRS will recover the funds.

In such cases, you can negotiate with the IRS to purchase the property using your own funds in return for a release of the lien. You might offer to pay a small fraction of the total amount owed. As the 120-day period nears its end, the possibility of significant discounts increases. It's important to note that the payment required is the remaining mortgage balance, not the potentially higher market value of the property.

Exhibit 5.12.7-1 Mutual Collection Assistance Request (MCAR) NFTL

Form **668(Y)**
(Rev. February 2004)

Department of the Treasury - Internal Revenue Service

Notice of Federal Tax Lien

Area:

Serial Number:
NNNNNNNN

For Optional Use by Recording Office

As provided by sections 6321, 6322, and 6323 of the Internal Revenue Code, we are giving a notice that taxes (including interest and penalties) have been assessed against the following-named taxpayer. We have made a demand for payment of this liability, but it remains unpaid. Therefore, there is a lien in favor of the United States on all property and rights to property belonging to this taxpayer for the amount of these taxes, and additional penalties, interest, and costs that may accrue.

Name of Taxpayer: *First Name Line*
Second Name Line

Address: *Street Address*
City, State ZIP

IMPORTANT RELEASE INFORMATION: For each assessment listed below, unless notice of lien is refiled by the date given in column (e), this notice shall, on the day following such date, operate as a certificate of release as defined in IRC 6325(a).

Kind of Tax (a)	Tax Period Ending (b)	Identifying Number (c)	Date of Assessment (d)	Last Day for Refiling (e)	Unpaid Balance of Assessment (f)
Income	*MM/DD/YYYY*	XXX-XX-*NNNN*	*MM/DD/YYYY*	*MM/DD/YYYY*	*NNN,NNN.NN*

****This amount is due, owing, and unpaid to the government of *[Treaty Partner]* and is being collected on behalf of *[Treaty Partner]* under the provisions of Article *[NN]* of the United States – *[Treaty Partner]* Income Tax Convention and applicable provisions of the Internal Revenue Laws of the United States****

Place of Filing: *Recording Official*
Recording Office
City, State

Total $ *NNN,NNN.NN*

This notice was prepared and signed at *City, State*, **on this,**

the *DD* **day of** *Month* , *YYYY* .

Signature:

Requestor's Name, Employee ID #

Title:

Phone #

(NOTE: Certificate of officer authorized by law to take acknowledgements is not essential to the validity of Notice of Federal Tax Lien, Rev. Rul. 71-466, 1971-2 C.B. 409)

Part 1 – Recording Office Form **668(Y)** (Rev 2-2004) Cat. No. 60025X

Image 7: IRS Form 668(Y): Federal Tax Lien

Judgment Liens: If a court issues a monetary judgment against a property owner, the plaintiff creditor who won the judgment can record a lien on the property's legal title. This lien enables the creditor to fulfill the judgment which includes statutory interest either by seizing the property or by obtaining proceeds from its sale. This represents another form of 'equitable' title interest. It's important to note that these liens automatically expire if there is a stealthy remainderman or a reversionary estate.

Homeowners Association (HOA) Liens: Homeowners associations have the authority to impose liens on properties for unpaid dues or assessments. These liens secure the association's claim on the property until the outstanding payments are settled.

Consensual Liens: Some liens are created voluntarily through mutual agreements between parties. For instance, a property owner might willingly grant a consensual lien to a lender or creditor as part of a secured transaction.

Lease Option Liens: If the lease and/or option is recorded with a mortgage or deed of trust as security any subsequent legal title transfer is then subject to the lessee/optionee's rights.

Franchise Tax Liens: These are filed against registered legal entities for unpaid taxes. California's Franchise Tax Board is very aggressive in collecting these taxes. You cannot formally dissolve a Corporation or LLC until the FTB account is settled.

Lis Pendens Liens: When a person seeks damages from another and there is either a direct claim against their property or a strong likelihood that the real property's value could be diminished or 'wasted' before the trial, a Lis Pendens Lien can be filed. This serves as a warning to potential buyers, lenders, or others that a future claim could be made against the property after a court decision.

This is a particularly vicious kind of lien because it prevents the defendant in the suit from being able to use this property as collateral to secure loans needed to fight the lawsuit. The purpose of a Lis Pendens is to safeguard any equity the plaintiff may have in the property, which could be subject to a judgment award. Hence, a Lis Pendens can act as a double-edged sword.

If a Lis Pendens is filed, the defendant can challenge its validity by presenting facts that question the merit of the case or show that the real property is unlikely to be 'wasted.'

If the Lis Pendens is deemed to have been filed frivolously or maliciously without any valid basis, and if the plaintiff loses the lawsuit and refuses to withdraw it, this action is seen as prima facie evidence that the Lis Pendens was intended more to obstruct the defense than for legitimate reasons. As a result, all involved parties on the losing side, including their attorneys, could be held personally liable.

Common Law Liens: This category includes innkeepers' liens which legally allow the seizure of a lodger's luggage to cover unpaid charges for accommodation. Additionally, common law liens enable citizens to file claims against government officials and large corporations, compelling them to address allegations of misconduct and negligence in court. However, this action is akin to a citizen's arrest and may lead to adverse outcomes over time.

Vendor/Vendee Liens: In certain jurisdictions, equitable liens arise when one party transfers property title under a contract that is later found to be deficient. These liens can be enforced through the process of foreclosure.

Bail Bond Liens: These refer to 'surety bonds' used to guarantee a court appearance secured against a property's equity. A non-refundable premium is paid for these bonds. Once the required court appearances are made and a court order for the release is issued and recorded, the process to release the lien can begin.

There are also various types of government and tax liens, including estate taxes, generation-skipping taxes, gift taxes, excise taxes, ad valorem taxes, and special assessment liens. Additionally, liens can result from zoning violations or judgment liens arising from legal awards at the city, county, state, regional, or federal levels. The frequency of these liens is likely to increase due to self-funding agencies like the EPA and cases involving the Racketeer Influenced and Corrupt Organizations (RICO) Act.

Lien Removal: They can be released by the party who recorded them if the associated debt is paid off, set aside by a court order, expire due to the statute of limitations (unless refiled promptly), extinguished by the termination of the estate against which they were filed, or through foreclosure proceedings.

It's essential for property owners and potential buyers to be aware of any existing liens on a property as they can directly impact the property's marketability and the ability to obtain financing.

Before selling or transferring ownership, clearing or resolving any liens is often necessary. Title searches and title insurance are frequently employed during the real estate escrow process to detect and manage potential liens effectively.

13
TITLE INSURANCE

Now we'll move onto title insurance which is designed to protect both buyers and lenders after a real property purchase transaction. It all began to take shape in 1874 after the Pennsylvania Supreme Court passed legislation authorizing title insurance. As you might imagine it was the result of a property buyer's loss and subsequent lawsuit. It was a necessary and logical solution.

American 'Real Property' law defines and regulates the acquisition, transfer, protection, and enforcement of ownership of RIGHTS and INTERESTS associated with realty.

Across the United States and most areas, people rely upon title insurance to protect them from the claims that might be raised by the Native American tribes. We've all heard of Spanish land grants emerging in California to challenge ownership and of lawsuits filed in New England to perfect Indian rights.

Title insurance is a form of indemnity insurance that protects lenders and homebuyers from financial loss sustained when title to a property is 'clouded' (not free & clear of defects). Unlike traditional insurance which protects against future events, title insurance covers events affecting the title that have occurred in the past.

The California Land Title Association (CLTA) and the American Land Title Association (ALTA) policies are two types of title insurance policies that cater to different needs and legal standards across the United States.

CLTA policies typically provide basic title insurance coverage. They are designed to protect property owners and mortgage lenders against losses from certain defects in the title that are listed in the policy, such as forgery, fraud, and issues with the legal ownership of the property.

> "...title insurance covers events affecting the title that have occurred in the past."

As suggested by its name, the CLTA policy is tailored to meet the legal and transactional requirements specific to California. However, the principles of coverage are similar to basic title insurance policies found in other states.

In comparison, ALTA policies provide a more comprehensive range of coverages. They are designed to protect against a wider variety of risks including those related to the land's physical boundaries and location, such as encroachments, easements, and issues undiscovered in public records.

ALTA policies are designed to meet national standards, making them applicable and consistent across the United States. This makes ALTA policies a preferred choice for transactions involving lenders or properties in various states.

In Texas and other states, special types of policies are issued. New Yorkers usually wind up with title policies that are issued under the auspices of the New York Board of Title Underwriters. These aren't as comprehensive as ALTA policies. In Ohio, title policies ensure record title only and give no protection against off risk records such as forged deeds, fraudulent releases of mortgages, insanity, etc.

California issues policies under the California Land Title Association (CLTA) which generally rely upon tax maps for legal descriptions rather than surveys. California tax maps are less than reliable especially when buying acreage. There was once a ranch in California in which an accurate survey reflected a difference of 19 acres from the applicable tax maps.

It's essential to understand that with title insurance policies, the protections offered on the first page are often restricted by the details on the second page. Regardless of the initial promises, the insurer may exclude coverage for various issues it deems risky. Common exclusions typically cover rights of current property occupants, any environmental violations, the precise placement of fences, and any encroachments that a survey might disclose, along with any conditions that were known to the insured but not disclosed.

Furthermore, state laws often define a 'root of title,' which is considered the historical point from which legal ownership is assumed to be valid. However, this can pose risks. For instance, a person purchased 40 acres in Arkansas only to find out that a fraudulent deed had been filed back in 1909 after the previous owner's death, rendering all subsequent deeds void.

Title insurance is normally an integral component of the escrow process. They go together.

Homeowner — CLTA

Homeowners title insurance is a specialized policy designed to safeguard homeowners and lenders against potential problems with the property's title.

This form of insurance is different from standard homeowner's insurance, which generally protects against damage to the home's physical structure and the personal belongings inside it. Key Points include:

- Title Examination: Before a property is purchased, a title examination is conducted to verify the ownership history and ensure that the title is free from defects, liens, and other encumbrances. However, even with a thorough examination, hidden issues can arise later.

- Title Defects: Include undisclosed heirs, errors in public records, lawsuits, fraud, forgery, easements, or other issues that could threaten the homeowner's right to the property.

- One-Time Premium: Homeowners typically pay a one-time premium for title insurance at the time of closing the real estate transaction. The policy remains in effect for as long as the homeowner or their heirs have an interest in the property.

- Lender Requirement: Buyers are generally required by their lender to also purchase lender's title insurance. This policy does not protect the homeowner, only the lender.

- Coverage Limits: The coverage provided can have limits and the specific coverage can vary by policy. But it generally includes protection against undiscovered title defects, legal fees, and other costs associated with defending the title.

It's important for homebuyers to carefully read the terms and coverage of the title insurance policy. But it is not mandatory for all real estate transactions.

Other times I've seen cash buying investors only obtain a preliminary title report. If satisfied with risk assessment, they forgo buying title insurance. This is only for experts or special situations. But title insurance does eliminate risk and it creates valuable peace of mind. Here's one story:

Emily and Alex, who after years of saving, finally bought their dream home. The property had everything they wanted—a big backyard for their dog, a spacious kitchen, and a lovely view of a nearby park.

They were aware of the importance of title insurance and opted for a standard owner's title insurance policy as part of their closing process, feeling secure in their investment.

A few months after moving in, their peace was disrupted by a knock on the door. It was a man claiming to be the rightful owner of a portion of their backyard. He asserted that his grandfather had bought the land under a verbal agreement from the previous owner which was never formally recorded. He presented old, somewhat convincing documents.

Emily and Alex immediately contacted their title insurance company. The title insurance company took up their case, providing legal representation as part of their policy's coverage. The claim went to court, where it was revealed that the documents the man presented were indeed old but legally insignificant because there was no formal recording of the transaction. This also violates the Statute of Frauds, which requires real estate agreements in writing.

Title insurance provided Emily and Alex with legal defense and shielded them from any financial loss associated with defending their property rights. The court ruled in their favor, affirming their sole ownership of the property, including the disputed backyard area.

Lenders — ALTA

A lender's title insurance policy is a type of insurance that provides protection to lenders against financial loss that could result from defects in the title to a property. The lender's policy specifically protects the lender's interests up to the amount of the loan.

As previously explained, it's possible your homeowners title policy is optional but the lenders policy is mandatory. The lender has a vested and valuable equitable interest.

Although the CLTA policy previously mentioned has protections for a lender, they are only basic. This is why a more comprehensive ALTA policy is required.

Primary Function: To protect the mortgage or trust deed lender against financial losses or legal issues related to the property's title. It is meant to ensure that the lender's security interest in the property is valid and enforceable.

Coverage for Title Defects: The policy provides coverage for various title defects that may affect the lender's security interest such as undiscovered liens, errors in public records, undisclosed heirs, fraud, and other issues that could jeopardize the lender's claim to the property.

Required by Lenders: In most real estate transactions, lenders require the borrower to purchase a lender's title insurance policy. This requirement is often a standard part of the mortgage loan process.

One-Time Premium: The borrower typically pays a one-time premium for the lender's title insurance policy. The premium is typically based on the total loan amount and is more expensive (approx. 25%) than a CLTA policy.

This is because lenders require an additional cost survey and property inspection. The CLTA policy does not have these features.

Coverage Amount: The lender's title insurance policy is usually tied to the outstanding loan amount. As the borrower pays down the debt, the coverage amount decreases.

Policy Duration: The policy remains in effect for as long as the loan has an outstanding balance. Once it's paid off or refinanced the policy terminates. (See Image 8.)

American Land Title Association

Owner's Policy of Title Insurance
[2021 v. 01.00 (07-01-2021)]

ALTA OWNER'S POLICY OF TITLE INSURANCE
issued by
BLANK TITLE INSURANCE COMPANY

This policy, when issued by the Company with a Policy Number and the Date of Policy, is valid even if this policy or any endorsement to this policy is issued electronically or lacks any signature.

Any notice of claim and any other notice or statement in writing required to be given to the Company under this policy must be given to the Company at the address shown in Condition 17.

COVERED RISKS

SUBJECT TO THE EXCLUSIONS FROM COVERAGE, THE EXCEPTIONS FROM COVERAGE CONTAINED IN SCHEDULE B, AND THE CONDITIONS, [Blank Title Insurance Company], a [Blank] corporation (the "Company"), insures as of the Date of Policy and, to the extent stated in Covered Risks 9 and 10, after the Date of Policy, against loss or damage, not exceeding the Amount of Insurance, sustained or incurred by the Insured by reason of:

1. The Title being vested other than as stated in Schedule A.

2. Any defect in or lien or encumbrance on the Title. Covered Risk 2 includes, but is not limited to, insurance against loss from:
   a. a defect in the Title caused by:
      i. forgery, fraud, undue influence, duress, incompetency, incapacity, or impersonation;
      ii. the failure of a person or Entity to have authorized a transfer or conveyance;
      iii. a document affecting the Title not properly authorized, created, executed, witnessed, sealed, acknowledged, notarized (including by remote online notarization), or delivered;
      iv. a failure to perform those acts necessary to create a document by electronic means authorized by law;
      v. a document executed under a falsified, expired, or otherwise invalid power of attorney;
      vi. a document not properly filed, recorded, or indexed in the Public Records, including the failure to have performed those acts by electronic means authorized by law;
      vii. a defective judicial or administrative proceeding; or
      viii. the repudiation of an electronic signature by a person that executed a document because the electronic signature on the document was not valid under applicable electronic transactions law.
   b. the lien of real estate taxes or assessments imposed on the Title by a governmental authority due or payable, but unpaid.
   c. the effect on the Title of an encumbrance, violation, variation, adverse circumstance, boundary line overlap, or encroachment (including an encroachment of an improvement across the boundary lines of the Land), but only if the encumbrance, violation, variation, adverse circumstance, boundary line overlap, or encroachment would have been disclosed by an accurate and complete land title survey of the Land.

3. Unmarketable Title.

4. No right of access to and from the Land.

Image 8: ALTA Owner's Policy of Title Insurance

Deeds — Legal Title

A deed is a written instrument that conveys legal title from one person to another.

There are various types of deeds. The two most popular are Warranty deed and Grant Deed. Both serve to transfer ownership rights from the seller (grantor) to the buyer (grantee). However they come with different levels of protection and guarantees for the buyer.

All deeds must be in writing per the Statute of Frauds. They must include the name of the grantor and grantee, a full legal description of the property (lot number, block, subdivision, map, book page, county, etc). This is different from the street address or assessor's parcel number (APN). The deed must include 'conveyance' words, e.g., grant, bargain, sell, convey. The grantor (seller) must sign the deed in front of a notary to have it recorded. The grantee (buyer) does not sign the deed. The deed must have a date.

Many escrow and title companies handling your transaction now require their own in-house notaries to acknowledge deeds. This is to prevent fraud and provide safety.

Warranty Deed

Full Protection: A warranty deed provides the highest level of protection to the buyer. It guarantees that the property is free from any liens, debts, or other encumbrances that weren't disclosed at the time of sale. This type of deed has the most liability for a seller.

Title Guarantees: The seller using a warranty deed guarantees they have the legal right to sell the property and that the title is clear. This includes a promise to defend the buyer against any future claims to the property.

Covenants Included: Warranty deeds typically include several covenants or guarantees about the property's status. For example, the covenant of seisin (guaranteeing the grantor's ownership and legal right to sell), the covenant against encumbrances, and the covenant of quiet enjoyment (ensuring the grantee won't be disturbed by third-party title claims).

Grant Deed – Western States

Limited Protection: A grant deed offers less protection than a warranty deed. It only guarantees that the property hasn't been sold to someone else and that there are no undisclosed liens or encumbrances at the time of transfer, based on the seller's knowledge.

No Future Claims Protection: Unlike a warranty deed, a grant deed does not protect the buyer against future claims. If there are issues with the title that arise after the sale, the seller is not obligated to defend the buyer. This is one reason you get title insurance.

Implied Guarantees: The main guarantees are that the seller has not conveyed the property to someone else prior to you, and that the property is being transferred without hidden encumbrances.

Key Differences Summary

Level of Guarantee and Protection: Warranty deeds provide comprehensive protection against claims and encumbrances. Grant deeds offer implied covenants primarily ensuring no prior conveyances or hidden encumbrances by the grantor.

Warranty deeds do include a guarantee to defend the buyer's title against future claims.

Grant deeds do not include a guarantee to defend the buyer's title against future claims.

Use Cases: Warranty deeds are commonly used in residential property transactions across many states, offering buyers peace of mind. Grant deeds are more common in certain states like California and Nevada. They're used when the seller is willing to guarantee certain aspects of the title but not to the extent of a warranty deed.

Buyers often prefer warranty deeds for the comprehensive protection they offer, but in some markets or situations, like the state of California, a grant deed is considered sufficient. No matter what type of deed is used, title insurance protects homeowners and lenders.

NOTE: Either type of deed represents a change in legal title ownership. When recorded, this event can trigger property tax re-assessments, transfer taxes or stamp duty.

Public Recording

Although you must execute real estate transactions in writing to be valid, there is no legal requirement they be publicly recorded. Technically, you can have a grant deed signed by the seller made out to you. No recording. No notary. But transfer (conveyance) of legal title has occurred.

However, it is safer to record deeds representing ownership transfers. Lenders will always require recording. A notary's acknowledgement is required too.

14
TITLE & LIEN FRAUD

In order to protect your assets, you need to be aware of the risk of title fraud.

Most of us are aware of personal identity theft. A similar concept applies to real estate. Here a thief desires to steal financial benefits from the true property owner. Their efforts may succeed or fail depending upon a variety of factors you need to know. When that happens, it becomes title fraud.

> "Title fraud is also known as deed fraud or property title fraud. This occurs when someone illegally alters ownership or the title of a property without the homeowner's consent."

Title fraud is also known as deed fraud or property title fraud. This occurs when someone illegally alters ownership or the title of a property without the homeowner's consent.

Thieves appropriate a homeowners SSN or driver's license. Then they transfer the property title to the fraudster's name or business entity. Forged documents and the submission of false information is what happens next.

The fraudster can then secure loans against the property, leaving the legitimate homeowner liable for the debts. Or they can attempt to sell the property without the homeowner's knowledge. This can have devastating financial and legal consequences for the victim. One easy target is rarely used second homes.

Title fraud is a criminal offense and those found guilty face legal consequences. Resolving title fraud is painful as it's a complex and time-consuming process.

The problem is that no property owner inspects the Recorder's records on a daily basis. After buying a property few people ever think of or are aware of title fraud risk. We rarely ever had this problem in the past.

Here's a story from Toronto, January 2022. Two thieves used fake identification to pose as the homeowners of a vacant house. Then they listed the property for sale with a real estate broker. The property sold, title and money was exchanged, new homeowners took possession. The money and thieves are nowhere to be found. Can you imagine this scene? It's a mess.

An elderly man (95 yo) was moving to long-term care and the family was in charge of renting out his former home. The prospective tenants used fake documents and references for the lease. Then someone took over the old guys identity and tried to sell the house. The family got lucky and aborted the scam.

Another property owner in Las Vegas used his LLC for holding title. Thieves realized this $5m vacant land was free & clear by searching the Clark County Recorder's records. Then they hacked the LLC's Secretary of State (SOS) online account and replaced the manager. Subsequently they obtained a loan — bingo. Escrow and title blames SOS records. The SOS says we're not responsible. Another big legal money nightmare.

In San Diego a mentally ill man submitted a properly filled out grant deed to the county Recorder. The deed transferred legal title from the PETCO Baseball Park to him. The Recorder's staff is barred from passing judgment on whether a recording is correct. There is no system to verify if a notary endorsement is forged or valid. If a deed is filled out in compliance with recording requirements, the clerk is obliged to process it.

Thieves search property records for equity – those without a mortgage. This makes the escrow process much easier and faster. Sometimes petty criminals are paid $10k as nominees to 'become the homeowner' and sign documents. The real fraudsters are never identified and get the big money.

It's crucial for property owners to regularly monitor their property records and purchase title insurance as a protective measure. Although title insurance can't prevent title fraud, it can cover the legal costs to restore title.

There are also 'title monitoring' services that will notify you of any title changes from the Recorder's office. You can find many of them online.

However, title lock or notifications from the recorder of a document being recorded is too late! It's already happened and now you must take affirmative action to unravel the mess. This generally means hiring a real estate lawyer.

Or you can choose prevention. Rather than the standard ALTA 'owners' policy, pay 10% more and get a 'homeowners' policy. This will cover you in the event of forgery or impersonation after the policy is issued. This is very much a little known secret.

American Land Title Association

Homeowner's Policy of Title Insurance
[2021 v. 01.01 (07-01-2021 TC 09-21-2021)]

ALTA HOMEOWNER'S POLICY OF TITLE INSURANCE
issued by
BLANK TITLE INSURANCE COMPANY

This policy, when issued by Us with a Policy Number and the Date of Policy, is valid even if this policy or any endorsement to this policy is issued electronically or lacks any signature.

As soon as You Know of anything that might be covered by this policy, You must notify Us promptly in writing at the address shown in Condition 3.

COVERAGE STATEMENT

SUBJECT TO THE PROVISIONS SET FORTH BELOW, We insure You against loss or damage resulting from one or more of the Covered Risks if the matter creating the risk exists on the Date of Policy or, to the extent expressly stated in any Covered Risk, after the Date of Policy. We will also pay the costs, attorneys' fees, and expenses provided for under this policy.

Your insurance is effective on the Date of Policy.

This policy covers You only if the Land is improved with an existing one-to-four family residence and each party named in Item 1 of Schedule A is a Natural Person or Estate Planning Entity.

Your insurance is further limited by all of the following:

- Amount of Insurance
- For Covered Risks 16, 18, 19, and 21, Your Deductible Amount and Our Maximum Dollar Limit of Liability shown in Schedule A
- Exceptions from Coverage in Schedule B
- Our Duty to Defend against Legal Actions
- Exclusions from Coverage
- Conditions

COVERED RISKS

1. Someone else owns an interest in Your Title.
2. Someone else has a right affecting Your Title because of a lease, contract, or option.
3. Someone else claims to have a right affecting Your Title because of forgery or impersonation.
4. Someone else has an Easement on the Land.
5. Any of Covered Risks 1 through 4 occurring after the Date of Policy.
6. Someone else has a right to enforce a Covenant to limit Your use of the Land.
7. Your Title is defective. Some examples of title defects are:
    a. someone else's failure to have authorized a transfer or conveyance of Your Title.
    b. a defective judicial or administrative proceeding.

Image 9: ALTA Homeowners Policy of Title Insurance

Personal Property – AKA Chattel

Chattel is personal property. Here we'll discuss personal property. Ownership and liens use the same concepts as real estate. However, the documents and processes are different.

So what is personal property or chattel? It's anything other than real property (estate).

Personal property can be tangible or intangible.

Tangible property has physical form. You can touch it. You can move it. For example, clothes, vehicles, boats, aircraft, construction cranes, manufactured homes, firearms, livestock, jewelry, furniture, etc.

Intangible property only exists on paper. These are often financial assets. For example, bank or brokerage account, pensions, patents and trademarks, currency, stock or shares in a company, etc.

Either type (tangible or intangible) of personal property is 'movable.' You can take it with you to another street, building, city, state, country.

In legal terms, personal property is also referred to as "personalty" (yes, without the i.)

Title Transfers

Ownership transfers with real property is a deed. Depending upon the value or payment made these transactions can trigger disclosures, sales taxes or transfer taxes.

With personal property you typically use a "bill of sale" to change legal title when there is a bona fide sale and purchase.

For investment or estate planning purposes you might also use an 'assignment' for transferring legal title. In many cases there is no consideration (exchange of value). For example, shares of a company owned in your personal name which are transferred to your living trust.

Government agencies with oversight or control of select assets have their own policies and compliance requirements. Think of vehicles, aircraft, or watercraft. For example, the DMV, USPTO or FAA. They have in-house forms you must complete to provide written evidence of a transfer which then results in a legal title change.

15
VESTING TITLE – PERSONAL PROPERTY

You can use a personal name, joint ownership, business organization, or a trust in order to vest title on personal property. Here are a few examples:

- Individual Name – single person ownership.
- Joint Owners (and/or) – two or more people.
- John Smith and Lorena Sanchez. That means both parties need to sign off the title for any transfers.
- John Smith or Lorena Sanchez. That means either party can sign off the title for any transfers.

Corporation (Inc) – an organization sanctioned by the state owning any type of personal property.

Limited Liability Company (LLC) – a state entity which can own any type of personal property.

Living Trust – an instrument to distribute your estate. Ideal for holding a personal residence, stocks, bonds, non-retirement accounts, savings.

Example: Smith Family Living Trust, DTD 01/01/2023, Jack Smith as Trustee

Personal Property Trust – these types of trusts are NOT for real estate or operating a business. Their sole purpose is for holding title to personal property assets. The main benefit is title privacy. Additional benefits include probate avoidance and possibly judgment protection.

Example: Cook Trust, Jack Smith as Trustee.

Business Trust Company – this trust can hold both real and personal property. The benefits include privacy, asset protection, probate avoidance, etc.

Example: Helena Investment Company.

> "You can use a personal name, joint ownership, business organization, or a trust in order to vest title on personal property."

Exceptions:

Pension Plans – these are generally titled in the name of an individual. This is because tax sensitive accounts are tied to a single taxpayer and their SSN. You may select any variety of beneficiaries, but the pension plan legal title owner is almost always an individual.

Bank/Brokerage Accounts – there is an alternative to a will or trust for estate planning. Provide your banker with 'Payable on Death' (POD) instructions. This means your account is automatically transferred 'after death' to a specific beneficiary(ies). Each institution has its own forms and requirements. If practical, introduce your beneficiary(ies) to the banker in person.

For brokerage accounts it's often known as 'Transfer on Death' (TOD) instructions. This is for stocks, bonds, and other investment assets.

Your heirs will own these accounts without any obligations to your estate. Beneficiaries have no rights or control of your accounts while living. You may amend or cancel POD/TOD instructions at any time.

16
PERSONAL PROPERTY LIENS

When any type of personal property (tangible or intangible) is pledged as security for a promise, it is common for lenders within the US to subscribe to the Uniform Commercial Code.

Personal property contracts that exceed $500 in value are also subject to the Statute of Frauds. This means those transactions must be in writing for validity.

The Uniform Commercial Code (UCC) is a set of standardized regulations adopted by all 50 states for conducting business and financial transactions with chattel or personal property.

> "Personal property contracts that exceed $500 in value are also subject to the Statute of Frauds."

When personal property is pledged as security for a promise (loan) a financing statement is created, evidenced by form UCC-1 filed with the state and county to notify the public of a lenders security interest. The property is 'collateralized.'

But there are exceptions where debt consolidation and home improvement loans are secured by both the real estate and attached list of personal property on a mortgage or deed of trust.

In such cases, the mortgage language states that the lien against the real estate remains until paid off completely or all the listed personal property, e.g., furniture has been conveyed along with the real property.

Lenders hold legal title during the entire term of loan. Only after paid off do they release the legal title to the buyer. Form UCC-3 is used to amend, assign, or terminate an existing UCC lien.

Compared to 30-year real estate loans, personal property or chattel loans have a short time frame. Car loans are 24-72 months. In addition, interest rates are higher. The original loan term is generally based upon the remaining economic life of the property.

Housing & Community Development (HCD) regulates and tracks ownership along with liens on manufactured housing. Their forms include title, registration, liens, etc.

The Federal Aviation Administration (FAA) has their own forms and registry of aircraft liens. Form 8050-98 is the Aircraft Security Agreement. Form 8050-2 is the Bill of Sale. (See Image 10.)

OMB Control No. 2120-0042
Exp. 03/31/2024

PRA Public Burden Statement: A federal agency may not conduct or sponsor, and a person is not required to respond to, nor shall a person be subject to a penalty for failure to comply with a collection of information subject to the requirements of the Paperwork Reduction Act unless that collection of information displays a currently valid OMB Control Number. The OMB Control Number for this information collection is 2120-0042. Public reporting for this collection of information is estimated to be approximately 45 minutes per response, including the time for reviewing instructions, searching existing data sources, gathering and maintaining the data needed, completing and reviewing the collection of information. All responses to this collection of information are required for recordation of security interest, in aircraft, engines, propellers and spare parts, in accordance with 14 CFR Part 49. Send comments regarding this burden estimate or any other aspect of this collection of information, including suggestions for reducing this burden to: Information Collection Clearance Officer, Federal Aviation Administration, 10101 Hillwood Parkway, Fort Worth, TX 76177-1524.

DEPARTMENT OF TRANSPORTATION
FEDERAL AVIATION ADMINISTRATION
CIVIL AVIATION REGISTRY
AIRCRAFT REGISTRATION BRANCH
P. O. Box 25504
Oklahoma City, Oklahoma 73125
AIRCRAFT SECURITY AGREEMENT

NAME & ADDRESS OF DEBTOR
NAME & ADDRESS OF SECURED PARTY/ASSIGNOR
ASSIGNED/NAME & ADDRESS OF ASSIGNEE

ABOVE SPACE
FOR FAA USE ONLY

Date: ____________________________

A security interest is hereby granted to the secured party on the following described collateral:
AIRCRAFT (FAA registration number, manufacturer, model, and serial number):

NOTICE: ENGINES LESS THAN 550 HORSEPOWER AND PROPELLERS NOT CAPABLE OF ABSORBING 750 OR MORE RATED SHAFT HORSEPOWER ARE NOT ELIGIBLE FOR RECORDING.

ENGINES (manufacturer, model, and serial number):

PROPELLERS (manufacturer, model, and serial number):

SPARE PARTS LOCATIONS (air carrier's name, city, and state):

together with all equipment and accessories attached thereto or used in connection therewith, including engines of ______ horsepower, or the equivalent, and propellers capable of absorbing ________ rated takeoff shaft horsepower, described above, all of which are included in the term aircraft as used herein.
The above described aircraft is hereby mortgaged to the secured party for the purpose of securing in the order named:

FIRST: The payment of all indebtedness evidenced by and according to the terms of that certain promissory note, herein below described, and all renewals and extensions thereof.

Note bearing date _________ executed by the debtor and payable to the order of ____________________________ in the aggregate sum of $________ with interest thereon at the rate of ___________ per centum per annum, from date, payable in installments as follows: The principal and interest of said note is payable in _______ installments of $ ________ each on ________day of each successive month beginning with the _______ day of _________ The last payment of $ _________ is due on the ________ day of __________

AC 8050-98 (04/21)

Image 10: FAA Security Agreement

For illustrative purposes only.
Click for the UCC-1 Financing Statement published by the California Secretary of State which may be filed.

UCC - 1 FINANCING STATEMENT
California (Rev. 04/20/11)

UCC FINANCING STATEMENT
FOLLOW INSTRUCTIONS

A. NAME & PHONE OF CONTACT AT FILER (optional)

B. E-MAIL CONTACT AT FILER (optional)

C. SEND ACKNOWLEDGMENT TO: (Name and Address)

THE ABOVE SPACE IS FOR FILING OFFICE USE ONLY

1. DEBTOR'S NAME: Provide only one Debtor name (1a or 1b) (use exact, full name; do not omit, modify, or abbreviate any part of the Debtor's name); if any part of the Individual Debtor's name will not fit in line 1b, leave all of item 1 blank, check here ☐ and provide the Individual Debtor information in item 10 of the Financing Statement Addendum (Form UCC1Ad)

1a. ORGANIZATION'S NAME				
OR 1b. INDIVIDUAL'S SURNAME	FIRST PERSONAL NAME	ADDITIONAL NAME(S)/INITIAL(S)		SUFFIX
1c. MAILING ADDRESS	CITY	STATE	POSTAL CODE	COUNTRY

2. DEBTOR'S NAME: Provide only one Debtor name (2a or 2b) (use exact, full name; do not omit, modify, or abbreviate any part of the Debtor's name); if any part of the Individual Debtor's name will not fit in line 2b, leave all of item 2 blank, check here ☐ and provide the Individual Debtor information in item 10 of the Financing Statement Addendum (Form UCC1Ad)

2a. ORGANIZATION'S NAME				
OR 2b. INDIVIDUAL'S SURNAME	FIRST PERSONAL NAME	ADDITIONAL NAME(S)/INITIAL(S)		SUFFIX
2c. MAILING ADDRESS	CITY	STATE	POSTAL CODE	COUNTRY

3. SECURED PARTY'S NAME (or NAME of ASSIGNEE of ASSIGNOR SECURED PARTY): Provide only one Secured Party name (3a or 3b)

3a. ORGANIZATION'S NAME				
OR 3b. INDIVIDUAL'S SURNAME	FIRST PERSONAL NAME	ADDITIONAL NAME(S)/INITIAL(S)		SUFFIX
3c. MAILING ADDRESS	CITY	STATE	POSTAL CODE	COUNTRY

4. COLLATERAL: This financing statement covers the following collateral:

5. Check only if applicable and check only one box: Collateral is ☐ held in a Trust (see UCC1Ad, item 17 and Instructions) ☐ being administered by a Decedent's Personal Representative

6a. Check only if applicable and check only one box: ☐ Public-Finance Transaction ☐ Manufactured-Home Transaction ☐ A Debtor is a Transmitting Utility

6b. Check only if applicable and check only one box: ☐ Agricultural Lien ☐ Non-UCC Filing

7. ALTERNATIVE DESIGNATION (if applicable): ☐ Lessee/Lessor ☐ Consignee/Consignor ☐ Seller/Buyer ☐ Bailee/Bailor ☐ Licensee/Licensor

8. OPTIONAL FILER REFERENCE DATA:

UCC FINANCING STATEMENT (Form UCC1) (Rev. 04/20/11)

PAGE 1 OF 2 — FORM 436-1 (UCC-1)

Image 11: UCC-1 Financial Statement

UCC FINANCING STATEMENT AMENDMENT

FOLLOW INSTRUCTIONS

A. NAME & PHONE OF CONTACT AT FILER (optional)

B. E-MAIL CONTACT AT FILER (optional)

C. SEND ACKNOWLEDGMENT TO: (Name and Address)

THE ABOVE SPACE IS FOR FILING OFFICE USE ONLY

1a. INITIAL FINANCING STATEMENT FILE NUMBER

1b. ☐ This FINANCING STATEMENT AMENDMENT is to be filed [for record] (or recorded) in the REAL ESTATE RECORDS
Filer: attach Amendment Addendum (Form UCC3Ad) and provide Debtor's name in item 13

2. ☐ TERMINATION: Effectiveness of the Financing Statement identified above is terminated with respect to the security interest(s) of Secured Party authorizing this Termination Statement

3. ☐ ASSIGNMENT (full or partial): Provide name of Assignee in item 7a or 7b, and address of Assignee in item 7c and name of Assignor in item 9
For partial assignment, complete items 7 and 9 and also indicate affected collateral in item 8

4. ☐ CONTINUATION: Effectiveness of the Financing Statement identified above with respect to the security interest(s) of Secured Party authorizing this Continuation Statement is continued for the additional period provided by applicable law

5. ☐ PARTY INFORMATION CHANGE:
Check one of these two boxes:
This Change affects ☐ Debtor or ☐ Secured Party of record
AND Check one of these three boxes to:
☐ CHANGE name and/or address: Complete item 6a or 6b; and item 7a or 7b and item 7c
☐ ADD name: Complete item 7a or 7b, and item 7c
☐ DELETE name: Give record name to be deleted in item 6a or 6b

6. CURRENT RECORD INFORMATION: Complete for Party Information Change - provide only one name (6a or 6b)

6a. ORGANIZATION'S NAME

OR

6b. INDIVIDUAL'S SURNAME	FIRST PERSONAL NAME	ADDITIONAL NAME(S)/INITIAL(S)	SUFFIX

7. CHANGED OR ADDED INFORMATION: Complete for Assignment or Party Information Change - provide only one name (7a or 7b) (use exact, full name; do not omit, modify, or abbreviate any part of the Debtor's name)

7a. ORGANIZATION'S NAME

OR

7b. INDIVIDUAL'S SURNAME

INDIVIDUAL'S FIRST PERSONAL NAME

INDIVIDUAL'S ADDITIONAL NAME(S)/INITIAL(S) | SUFFIX

7c. MAILING ADDRESS	CITY	STATE	POSTAL CODE	COUNTRY

8. ☐ COLLATERAL CHANGE: Also check one of these four boxes: ☐ ADD collateral ☐ DELETE collateral ☐ RESTATE covered collateral ☐ ASSIGN collateral

Indicate collateral:

9. NAME OF SECURED PARTY OF RECORD AUTHORIZING THIS AMENDMENT: Provide only one name (9a or 9b) (name of Assignor, if this is an Assignment)
If this is an Amendment authorized by a DEBTOR, check here ☐ and provide name of authorizing Debtor

9a. ORGANIZATION'S NAME

OR

9b. INDIVIDUAL'S SURNAME	FIRST PERSONAL NAME	ADDITIONAL NAME(S)/INITIAL(S)	SUFFIX

10. OPTIONAL FILER REFERENCE DATA:

UCC FINANCING STATEMENT AMENDMENT (Form UCC3) (Rev. 04/20/11)

Image 12: UCC-3 form

After Death Succession — Real Property

Once a property owner dies, their successor(s) is determined by how they held legal title. This also affects how quickly or slowly the transfer occurs.

- Sole Owner – heirs via will or probate
- Joint Tenants with Rights of Survivorship – surviving co-owner
- Community Property with Rights of Survivorship – surviving co-owner
- Community Property without Rights of Survivorship – heirs or estate of each owner
- Tenants in Common – heirs or estate of each owner

Current owner can also record a revocable TOD (transfer on death) deed. Avoids probate and living trust. Requires two witnesses. Must record within 60 days of notary date. (See Image 13.)

- LLC – depends upon membership agreement
- Living Trust – successor Trustee
- Land Trust – depends upon trust agreement
- Business Trust – depends upon trust agreement

NOTE: Existing mortgages or loans – remain an obligation of the surviving co-signer, estate, trust, or business. However, they are not 'personal' obligations of any heir. Preplanning your life insurance death benefit amount with the mortgage in mind is a smart move.

Recording requested by (name):

____

When recorded mail to
and mail tax statements to:

____

____

____

____

Recorder's Use Only

REVOCABLE TRANSFER ON DEATH (TOD) DEED

(California Probate Code Section 5642)

This document is exempt from documentary transfer tax under Rev. & Tax. Code § 11930. This document is exempt from preliminary change of ownership report under Rev. & Tax. Code § 480.3.

Assessor's Parcel No.: ____________________

Declaration of Exemption From Gov't Code § 27388.1 Fee

☐ Transfer is exempt from fee per GC § 27388.1(a)(2):
- ☐ recorded concurrently "in connection with" transfer subject to DTT
- ☐ recorded concurrently "in connection with" a transfer of residential dwelling to an owner-occupier

☐ Transfer is exempt from fee per GC 27388.1(a)(1):
- ☐ Fee cap of $225.00 reached ☐ Not related to real property

IMPORTANT NOTICE: THIS DEED MUST BE RECORDED ON OR BEFORE 60 DAYS AFTER THE DATE IT IS SIGNED AND NOTARIZED

Use this deed to transfer the residential property described below directly to your named beneficiaries when you die. YOU SHOULD CAREFULLY READ ALL OF THE INFORMATION ON THE OTHER PAGES OF THIS FORM. You may wish to consult an attorney before using this deed. It may have results that you do not want. Provide only the information asked for in the form. DO NOT INSERT ANY OTHER INFORMATION OR INSTRUCTIONS. This form MUST be RECORDED on or before 60 days after the date it is signed and notarized or it will not be effective.

PROPERTY DESCRIPTION

Print the legal description of the residential property affected by this deed:

____

____

____

BENEFICIARY(IES)

Name the person(s) or entity(ies) who will receive the described property on your death.

IF YOU ARE NAMING A PERSON, state the person's FULL NAME (DO NOT use general terms like "my children"). You may also wish to state the RELATIONSHIP that the person has to you (spouse, son, daughter, friend, etc.), but this is not required.

IF YOU ARE NAMING A TRUST, state the full name of the trust, the name of the trustee(s), and the date shown on the signature page of the trust.

IF YOU ARE NAMING A PRIVATE OR PUBLIC ENTITY, state the name of the entity as precisely as you can.

____

____

____

1

Image 13: Transfer on Death Deed

After Death Succession — Personal Property

Wait to notify the bank (think auto deposits & payments), utility companies (power & phone), or drive vehicles (insurance) of the deceased. Pause and think before acting. Once the estate administrator or trustee has all paperwork organized then proceed to address accounts and assets.

It's best not to drive the deceased vehicles until you're clear with the insurance company. The probate administrator, executor or successor trustee becomes the new 'temporary legal' title owner of all personal property assets pending final distribution to heirs.

Adding Heirs to Title

This is nearly always a mistake. Here's why. It's a one-way street. If you add heirs to your real estate or bank accounts, there is no reverse course. And it precludes tax benefits.

If you later want to remove this person from the title, that person must voluntarily sign a deed to reconvey their interest. Or they must voluntarily release their interest with the bank or brokerage company.

If there is an existing loan on property do the kids formally take on that obligation? Your heirs will forfeit step up in tax basis. If received after death, could have significant tax benefits.

Parents think of doing this for their kids but it creates problems. First is no step-up in tax basis. Second is you're at risk to kids financial affairs or problems because they now own a valuable asset. You could be removed from the property. You could also have new roommates. Potential for family conflicts. If you really want to give it before death, reserve yourself a life estate in the deed. This way you're protected.

Transfer on Death ("TOD") Beneficiary Claim Form

If you are the listed beneficiary on a TOD account, you can use this form to transfer or redeem your portion of the account to your name.

1. Current Account Information

First, please tell us about the account(s) that you wish to request the transfer or redemption from:

Full name of primary account owner ____________________ Date of death (mm/dd/yyyy) ____________

Full name of secondary account owner (if any) ____________________ Date of death (mm/dd/yyyy) ____________

Social Security Number ____________ Account number(s) ____________ Reference number (if applicable) ____________

2. Beneficiary Information

Please provide us with the following information about the beneficiary:

Individuals	Entities (Trust, Charity, Foundation, Business, etc.)
Full name of beneficiary	Full name of trust, foundation, estate, business entity etc.
Federal tax ID or Social Security number	Full name of trustee, authorized signer, partner, etc.
If the beneficiary is a minor, full name of responsible individual	Title (trustee, officer, executor, etc.) / Federal tax ID (entity's)
Date of birth (mm/dd/yyyy) / Contact telephone number	Date of trust (mm/dd/yyyy) / Contact telephone number
Street # / Street name	Street # / Street name
City / State / ZIP Code	City / State / ZIP Code

3. Instructions on Distributing the Beneficiary's Portion

As a listed beneficiary on a TOD account, you have the option to **redeem** or **transfer** your portion to a new or existing account in your name.

A) Transferring to a new or existing account

You may transfer your portion to a new or existing account with your name in the registration. To transfer your portion to a new account, please complete the appropriate **New Account Application**, and return it to us along with this completed form. Check the box below, and proceed to "Signatures".

☐ Please transfer my portion to a new account. I have enclosed a completed & signed New Account Application.

B) Redeeming Funds

To *redeem* your portion, complete the section below to tell us where to send your proceeds. For proper tax reporting, you must sign in **Section 4**. Please ensure that all information for you in **Section 2** is correct.

Image 14: Transfer on Death Form

Bankruptcy Impact on Title

Filing personal bankruptcy requires full disclosure of your assets, no matter how you hold legal title, e.g., personal name, Corporation, GP, LP, LLC, or Trust, etc.

Bankruptcy is actually an irrevocable trust itself. After filing, the federal bankruptcy 'trustee' becomes the legal title owner of your assets. It's a one way street.

Control of your assets has legally shifted from you to another person, the bankruptcy trustee. She/he is then directed by the bankruptcy court how to administer and settle the case of your assets and obligations.

However, assets that you have permanently given away with certain types of trusts may be excluded from bankruptcy administration. But a lookback period is determined by the type of BK filing and your state laws.

Contingent future title interests pose an interesting dilemma for the court.

Judgement Impact on Title

If you are sued in the court system and ultimately found obligated to pay there are ways legal title to your assets are impacted. Short of paying off the obligation, creditors may place liens against your real and personal property. Real estate is the first choice. If the judgment lien remains unpaid, a creditor can force the sale of your personal residence. (See Image 15.)

JUD-100

ATTORNEY OR PARTY WITHOUT ATTORNEY *(Name, state bar number, and address):* TELEPHONE NO.: FAX NO. *(Optional):* EMAIL ADDRESS *(Optional):* ATTORNEY FOR *(Name):*	*FOR COURT USE ONLY*
SUPERIOR COURT OF CALIFORNIA, COUNTY OF STREET ADDRESS: MAILING ADDRESS: CITY AND ZIP CODE: BRANCH NAME:	
PLAINTIFF: DEFENDANT:	
JUDGMENT ☐ **By Clerk** ☐ **By Default** ☐ **After Court Trial** ☐ **By Court** ☐ **On Stipulation** ☐ **Defendant Did Not Appear at Trial**	CASE NUMBER:

JUDGMENT

1. ☐ **BY DEFAULT**
   a. Defendant was properly served with a copy of the summons and complaint.
   b. Defendant failed to answer the complaint or appear and defend the action within the time allowed by law.
   c. Defendant's default was entered by the clerk upon plaintiff's application.
   d. ☐ **Clerk's Judgment** (Code Civ. Proc., § 585(a)). Defendant was sued only on a contract or judgment of a court of this state for the recovery of money.
   e. ☐ **Court Judgment** (Code Civ. Proc., § 585(b)). The court considered
      (1) ☐ plaintiff's testimony and other evidence.
      (2) ☐ plaintiff's written declaration (Code Civ. Proc., § 585(d)).
2. ☐ **ON STIPULATION**
   a. Plaintiff and defendant agreed (stipulated) that a judgment be entered in this case. The court approved the stipulated judgment and
   b. ☐ the signed written stipulation was filed in the case.
   c. ☐ the stipulation was stated in open court ☐ the stipulation was stated on the record.
3. ☐ **AFTER COURT TRIAL.** The jury was waived. The court considered the evidence.
   a. The case was tried on *(date and time):*
      before *(name of judicial officer):*
   b. Appearances by:

☐ Plaintiff *(name each):*	☐ Plaintiff's attorney *(name each):*
(1)	(1)
(2)	(2)
☐ Continued on Attachment 3b.	
☐ Defendant *(name each):*	☐ Defendant's attorney *(name each):*
(1)	(1)
(2)	(2)
☐ Continued on Attachment 3b.	

   c. ☐ Defendant did not appear at trial. Defendant was properly served with notice of trial.
   d. ☐ A statement of decision (Code Civ. Proc., § 632) ☐ was not ☐ was requested.

Page 1 of 2

Form Approved for Optional Use
Judicial Council of California
JUD-100 [Rev. January 1, 2024]

JUDGMENT

Code of Civil Procedure, §§ 585, 664.6

Image 15: Judgment Lien

Prenups Impact on Title

Any property (real estate, bank accounts, vehicles) or obligations (mortgage, cc debt, auto loans, student loans) you take on individually prior to legal marriage remain your responsibility.

Obligations of your future spouse remain separate. Just because you get married that does not mean that your pre-marital obligations automatically attach to new spouse. Important!

However, property or credit acquired after marriage will impact both spouses. Any credit 'jointly' signed after marriage is the obligation of both. But you can individually apply for credit w/o spouse as co-signer. If one spouse dies, the other remains liable.

A prenup is generally designed to reaffirm property owned before marriage and the disposition of property acquired during marriage.

NOTE: This does not apply to religious marriage. It does apply to legal marriage.

Divorce Impact on Title

Pre-marital assets owned by an individual and never co-mingled with a spouse while married generally remain sole and separate property.

However, any jointly owned marital property would need a voluntary resolution between the two divorcing spouses.

CONCLUSION

As you can see, *title* to any given asset has considerable depth and breadth. History is evidence of its importance to society.

Legal title is what most people gravitate toward when thinking about ownership of assets. There are many formats for holding legal title. A single individual, married couple, co-tenants or maybe a business. Each one has different objectives along with benefits and restrictions.

Deeper still is equitable title. These individuals or businesses do not necessarily own legal title to a property but they have an equity interest. For example, a lender that uses the asset as collateral. In the event the loan goes into default a lender can sell the collateral to recoup their money from a borrower. Think foreclosure or repossession.

There are unique asset protection and tax reduction strategies available with equitable title trust shares for real estate. Anonymity is safety. Few people ever know about or see the results of these secret behind the curtain events.

We also see a distinction between real property (real estate) and personal property (bank accounts, vehicles, etc) assets.

Personal financial situations such as death, prenups, bankruptcy, divorce or civil judgments can impact legal or equitable title.

Estate planning should include potential tax consequences as well as future events. This is because assets change, beneficiaries change, unplanned events occur.

Documents such as deeds are highly important as they convey or prove legal ownership. Recorded liens are evidence or security for a debt. Both are normally public information.

In conclusion, understanding the dimensions of title is powerful. You're more knowledgeable. You're aware of the constraints and opportunities. Create solutions that serve you best. And above all use trusts. Reach out anytime.

James Billings
Buenos Aires Argentina
20 September 2024

A PERSONAL NOTE FROM JAMES

Before finishing the book I'd like to write this personal note for the readers. How is it that I know so much about title and liens for assets? Let's read on…

My background includes a university degree in Economics followed by professional credentials in Aviation, Securities and Real Estate. In each field the rules of legal title is essentially important to various stakeholders. By default most investors use LLCs for legal title but they have serious handicaps few recognize. As a result I focused on land and business trusts because of their unique equitable title advantages.

Acting as a broker on behalf of clients I learned the institutional side of title. Acting as a principal on behalf of myself I learned the client side of title. Now I have first-hand experience of both sides.

Institutions and advisors have forced compliance regarding client privacy. But for clients who feel the impact of privacy its highly personal.

- Real Estate Broker – St Helena CA Wine Country
- Investor Buying & Selling Single Family Homes in San Diego by Knocking on Doors
- Single Handedly Raised $20,000,000 for Mobile Home Park Operator
- Pilot/Owner Cessna 320D
- Launched TrustArte 2011
- #1 Business Trust Video on YouTube
- Authored Book 'The Uncorporation' – bought by over 4,000 Amazon customers
- Invented the Business Trust e-Seminar, Estate Planning e-Seminar and Realty Trust e-Seminar

After seeing how title impacts the ownership of real and personal property I strongly advocate private trusts for higher value assets. This is because equitable title interests can protect you from unwanted liens and public disclosures. Standard title vesting is often compulsory but that's okay. The important point is knowing when to show and when to camouflage.

— James Billings

ABOUT THE AUTHOR

James is a global businessman. His professional credentials and success both touch valuable assets such as real estate, aircraft and business. Years ago he recognized the danger of internet search to "pull back the curtain" on your financial privacy. Today he provides solutions for clients who want their assets to remain unlisted or invisible. The key is "title" anonymity. James lives in San Diego and Buenos Aires.

Alphabetical Index

Made in the USA
Monee, IL
13 September 2026

62981964R00066